DUBLIN

The Complete Guide

Appletree Press

First published and printed by The Appletree Press Ltd,
19–21 Alfred Street, Belfast BT2 8DL.
Text © Hugh Oram, 1989, 1993, 1995.

This edition published in 1995.

A catalogue record for this book is
available from the British Library.

ISBN 0 86281 510 X

9 8 7 6 5 4 3 2

CONTENTS

INTRODUCTION

The city of Dublin is full of history and culture. With its plethora of historic monuments and places, the capital of Ireland has more of historic value and importance than any other city of its size in Europe. This guide lists all the major historic buildings and places, many redolent with the stirring events of Irish history.

Dublin has always been proud of its culture. Its literary tradition is recognised all over the world — Beckett, Joyce and Yeats to name but three of its most glittering literary stars. Contemporary literary residents include John Banville and Seamus Heaney. In recent years other aspects of culture have flourished in the capital: traditional Irish music, the visual arts (reflected in the burgeoning number of art galleries) and classical music, particularly since the advent of the National Concert Hall. On the rock music scene, Dublin has become internationally noted, with bands like U2 to the front of the world stage in recent years. The Temple Bar district is being developed as Dublin's cultural quarter, with substantial progress already made. Dublin has also seen many improvements on the shopping front, with further shopping centres and craft shops.

Few European capitals have a more natural setting, with the sea bordering the city, unspoiled countryside within a few minutes drive and to the immediate south of the city, a great range of hills, largely unspoiled and unpolluted. People who enjoy the 'buzz' of great cities and those who like open-air splendours and delights will find everything they wish in and around this lively and very human city, where strangers and visitors are made welcome.

HOW TO GET THERE

The city is easy to reach from abroad. From Britain, there are regular air services from London and the major provincial cities, while sea services connect Holyhead with Dublin and Dun Laoghaire. Daily sailings connect Cairnryan and Stranraer in Scotland with Belfast and Larne. Swansea is connected with Cork by regular ferry sailings. Regular sea services from mainland

Europe to Ireland also include extra services, starting in early 1995, between France and Ireland. For those countries with no direct air links to Dublin, there are frequent connections via London. Air access to Dublin from North America (Canada and the US) is improved with a greater number of flights offered by more airlines, via Shannon and London.

Within Dublin, the DART (Dublin Area Rapid Transit) provides a quick and frequent rail service linking the north and south sides of the city, running from Howth to Bray. There are frequent services between Dundalk and Arklow, Dublin and Maynooth, and Dublin and Kildare. Buses link all parts of the city, new CitySwift, Imp and Localink services have expanded the ranges. Although Dublin has some short motorways with more planned, driving is relatively easy, except in rush hours, but city-centre parking can be difficult.

TOURIST INFORMATION
Dublin Airport, ☎ 284 4768. *All year.*
Baggot St, Dublin 2 (Bord Failte HQ), ☎ 676 5871/661 6500. *April — end Oct.*
14 Upper O'Connell St, Dublin 1, ☎ 284 4768. *All year.*
Dun Laoghaire (St Michael's Wharf), ☎ 284 4768. *All year.*

WEATHER
Winters in Dublin are usually mild. Snow in the city is rare, although the Dublin Mountains can have quite heavy falls of snow. Summers are temperate. Temperatures of over 20°C are almost as rare as snow in winter. June is sometimes the sunniest month of the year, but Irish weather patterns change so frequently that it's impossible to make accurate long-term predictions. The average yearly rainfall total is very variable but usually it is about 800 mm. Relative humidity is usually between 70 and 90 per cent.

Average monthly temperatures (Centigrade)

J	F	M	A	M	J	J	A	S	O	N	D
5	5	6	8	11	13	15	14	13	10	7	6

ACCOMMODATION

Dublin has an excellent selection of accommodation for visitors, ranging from the very expensive (£££) £80 to £120 per person per night through expensive (££) £40 to £60, moderate (£) £30 to clean, friendly and homely guesthouses costing from £20 per person per night. Inexpensive accommodation, such as that run by *An Oige*, the Irish Youth Hostels Association, is also available, as are self-catering facilities. Stars in brackets denote tourist board designation: under the new system, hotels have one to five stars, guesthouses one to four.

HOTELS
£££
Berkeley Court (*****), *Lansdowne Rd, Dublin 4,* ☎ *660 1711*. In Ballsbridge area; two restaurants, luxury bar, health club facilities, shops, hairdresser.
Burlington (****), *Upper Leeson St, Dublin 4,* ☎ *660 5222*. Just S of city centre. Two restaurants, elaborately refurbished bar.
Conrad (*****), *Earlscourt Terrace, Dublin 2,* ☎ *676 5555*. Luxuriously comfortable, American-style hotel with friendly, efficient service. Downstairs Alfie Byrne bar, two fine restaurants.
Davenport (****), *Lr Merrion St, Dublin 2,* ☎ *661 6800*. In converted Plymouth Brethren church hall, with fascinating lobby, the last word in luxury.
Hibernian (****), *Eastmoreland Place, Dublin 4,* ☎ *668 7666*. Former nurses' home sumptuously converted, restaurant.
Jury's (*****), *Ballsbridge, Dublin 4,* ☎ *660 5000*. Spacious lobby with well-stocked shop leads into hotel proper with two restaurants and Coffee Dock grill, open 22½ hours daily. Dubliners' Bar is packed with memorabilia. Heated outdoor swimming pool. **The Towers,** beside the original hotel, is very exclusive, very expensive and very comfortable. Same telephone number as Jury's, entrance from Lansdowne Road.
Kildare Hotel and Country Club (*****), *Straffan, Co Kildare,* ☎ *627 3333*. The last word in pampered luxury with memorable

cuisine, within easy reach of Dublin.

Shelbourne (*****), *St Stephen's Green, Dublin 2,* ☎ *676 6471.* Dublin's oldest hotel, dating back more than 150 years, but recently refurbished. Restaurant, two bars. Lounge is *the* place for afternoon tea.

Westbury (*****), *off Grafton St, Dublin 2,* ☎ *679 1122.* Modern luxury hotel, a little characterless, but comfortable. Restaurants, bar, shop.

££

Ashling (***), *Parkgate St, Dublin 8,* ☎ *677 2324.* Modern, rather plain, hotel with bar, restaurant, near Heuston Station.

Blooms (***), *Anglesea St, Dublin 2,* ☎ *671 5622.* Centrally located, bar, restaurant. Rooms are modern and plainly styled.

Buswells (***), *Molesworth St, Dublin 2,* ☎ *676 4013.* Long established hotel, comfortable and friendly. Bar, restaurant.

Central (***), *Exchequer St, Dublin 2,* ☎ *679 7302.* Very well refurbished, very comfortable.

Doyle Montrose (***), *Stillorgan Rd, Dublin 4,* ☎ *269 3311.* Large modern hotel. Bar, restaurant, shop.

Doyle Skylon (***), *Drumcondra Rd, Dublin 9,* ☎ *837 9121.* Large modern hotel in same group as Montrose and Tara. Bar, restaurant, shop.

Doyle Tara (***), *Merrion Rd, Dublin 4,* ☎ *269 4666.* Modern hotel, recently extended. Bar, restaurant, shop. Rooms at front have fine views over Dublin Bay.

Fitzpatrick's Killiney Castle (****), *Killiney, Co Dublin,* ☎ *284 0700.* Modern, comfortable facilities adjacent to Dun Laoghaire Ferryport.

Forte Crest (****), *Dublin Airport,* ☎ *844 4211.* Modern hotel with bar, restaurant, shop, beside airport.

Grafton Plaza, *Johnson's Court, near Grafton St, Dublin 2,* ☎ *475 0888.* New hotel with comfortable rooms, Mexican theme bar and restaurant.

Killiney Court (***), *Killiney, Co Dublin,* ☎ *285 1622.* Plenty of facilities, including bar, two restaurants. Spectacular Dublin

Bay views, easy access from city by DART.

Longfields (***), *9-10 Lr Fitzwilliam St, Dublin 2,* ☎ *676 1367.* Georgian houses comfortable converted, centrally located.

Mont Clare (***), *Lr Merrion St, Dublin 2,* ☎ *661 6799.* Modern, comfortable hotel with bar and restaurant. Near back of Trinity College.

Regency (***), *Swords Rd, Dublin 9,* ☎ *837 3544.* Comfortable hotel adjacent to airport.

Royal Dublin (***), *O'Connell St, Dublin 1,* ☎ *873 3666.* Modern city centre hotel, bar, restaurant.

Royal Marine (***), *Dun Laoghaire, Co Dublin,* ☎ *280 1911.* Old established hotel, well refurbished, very convenient to Dun Laoghaire Ferryport.

Russell Court (***), *21-23 Harcourt St, Dublin 2,* ☎ *478 4066.* Well placed for St Stephen's Green and Grafton St.

Sachs (***), *Morehampton Rd, Dublin 4,* ☎ *668 0995.* On S side of city centre, bar, restaurant.

Temple Bar (***), *Fleet St, Dublin 2,* ☎ *677 3333.* Modern hotel, well furnished, comfortable rooms. Large stylish restaurant and bar, very convenient for city centre.

£

Barry's (**), *1-2 Great Denmark St, Dublin 1,* ☎ *874 6943.* Long established hotel, off Parnell Sq. Bar, restaurant.

Clarence (**), *6-8 Wellington Quay, Dublin 2,* ☎ *677 6178.* Old hotel well refurbished, modern bar, restaurant.

Clifton Court (*), *11 Eden Quay, Dublin 1,* ☎ *874 3535.* All standard facilities, right in city centre.

Hollybrook (**), *Howth Rd, Dublin 3,* ☎ *833 6623.* Near city centre, recently refurbished with bar, restaurant.

Jury's Christchurch Inn (***), *Christchurch Place, Dublin 8,* ☎ *475 0111.* All modern hotel facilities at economical price.

Lansdowne (**), *27 Pembroke Rd, Dublin 4,* ☎ *668 2522.* Well placed, recently refurbished. Bar, restaurant.

Leeson Court (**), *26-27 Lr Leeson St, Dublin 2,* ☎ *676 3380.* Comfortable, centrally situated, interesting bar.

Ormond (**), *Upper Ormond Quay, Dublin 7*, ☎ *872 1811*. Well refurbished, front rooms have good river views.

Orwell Lodge (*), *77 Orwell Rd, Rathgar, Dublin 6*, ☎ *497 7256*. Comfortable hotel in southern suburbs. Good restaurant.

Travelodge (**), *Swords, Co Dublin*, ☎ *840 9233*. Same chain as Forte Airport Hotel. Recently built budget accommodation with inexpensive restaurant.

Wellington Hotel (**), *21-22 Wellington Quay, Dublin 2*, ☎ *677 9315*. New budget hotel.

Wynn's (**), *38-39 Lr Abbey St, Dublin 1*, ☎ *874 5131*. Old-fashioned, but homely and right in city centre.

GUESTHOUSES

Anglesea Town House (****), *63 Anglesea Rd, Dublin 4*, ☎ *668 3877*.

Antrim Arms (**), *27B, Upper Drumcondra Rd, Dublin 9*, ☎ *837 5356*.

Ariel House (****), *52 Lansdowne Rd, Dublin 4*, ☎ *668 5512*.

Glenveagh (***), *31 Northumberland Rd, Dublin 4*, ☎ *668 4612*.

Grey Door (****), *22-23 Upper Pembroke St, Dublin 2*, ☎ *676 3286*.

Iona House (***), *5 Iona Park, Dublin 9*, ☎ *830 6217*.

Kilronan House (***), *70 Adelaide Rd, Dublin 2*, ☎ *475 5266*.

Kingswood Country House (***), *Naas Rd, Dublin 22*, ☎ *459 2428*.

Mount Herbert (***), *Herbert Rd, Dublin 4*, ☎ *668 4321*.

Raglan Lodge (****), *10 Raglan Rd, Ballsbridge, Dublin 4*, ☎ *660 6697*.

Ron's (*), *51 Clontarf Rd, Dublin 3*, ☎ *833 4985*.

St Jude's (**), *17 Pembroke Park, Ballsbridge, Dublin 4*, ☎ *668 0483*.

Tramore (**), *272 South Circular Rd, Dublin 8*, ☎ *454 2183*.

Uppercross (***), *26-30 Upper Rathmines Rd, Dublin 6*, ☎ *497 5486*.

HOSTELS

An Oige, the Irish Youth Hostels Association, runs a modern hostel with restaurant, offering cheap, overnight accommodation, at *61 Mountjoy St, Dublin 7,* ☎ *830 1600.* Outside Dublin, its nearest hostel is at Enniskerry, ☎ *286 4036/7.*

Avalon House, *55 Aungier St, Dublin 2,* ☎ *475 0001.*

'Goin' My Way', *15 Talbot St, Dublin 1,* ☎ *878 8484.*

ISAAC'S, *2-5 Frenchman's Lane, Dublin 1,* ☎ *874 9321.*

Kinlay House, *2-12 Lord Edward St, Dublin 2,* ☎ *679 6644.*

Marlborough Hostel, *81-82 Marlborough St, Dublin 1,* ☎ *874 7629.*

Morehampton House, *78 Morehampton Rd, Donnybrook, Dublin 4,* ☎ *668 8866.*

Old School House, *Eblana Avenue, Dun Laoghaire, Co Dublin,* ☎ *280 8777.*

YWCA, *Radcliff Hall, St John's Rd, Sandymount, Dublin 4,* ☎ *269 4521.* Budget accommodation for women.

SELF CATERING

Self-catering premises registered with Bord Failte, either flats or houses, can be booked through Tourist Information Offices.

Stephen's Hall, *14-17 Lr Leeson St, Dublin 2,* ☎ *661 0585,* is centrally located.

Trident Holiday Homes, *2 Sandymount Village Centre, Dublin 4,* ☎ *668 3534,* has many self-catering houses in the Dublin area for short term rental.

Trinity College, ☎ *677 2941,* **University College,** ☎ *706 7777* and **St Patrick's College,** *Maynooth,* ☎ *628 5222,* all rent reasonably priced accommodation during the summer vacation.

OTHER ACCOMMODATION

Tourist Information Offices will book accommodation and provide information on a wide selection of private houses in the Dublin area, plus camping and caravanning sites.

ANCIENT MONUMENTS

Despite the rapid expansion of the city over the last 30 years, Dublin still has interesting and carefully preserved ancient monuments, the last relics of a long-vanished social order. The two most impressive sites, Brugh na Boinne (including Newgrange, Knowth and Dowth) and Glendalough, are located some distance from Dublin. Visits to these impressive sites make fascinating day trips.

Baldongan, *6 km (4 miles) S of Skerries.* Remains of 15c church. Ruins of 13th c fortress; fine views from top of tower. *33 bus from city centre to Lusk, then 2.5 km (1.5 miles).*

Brenanstown, *Carrickmines, Co Dublin.* Glen Druid dolmen, one of the largest stone remnants of prehistoric Ireland. *86 bus from city centre to Carrickmines.*

Brugh na Boinne, *11 km (7 miles) W of Drogheda, just S of N51 to Slane.* Within this 15 sq km area there are at least 15 passage graves. The most striking are Newgrange, Knowth and Dowth. Newgrange, probably dating from 2,500 BC, is one of the finest passage graves in W Europe. Building work required nearly 200,000 tons of stone. ☎ *(041) 24488.* New interpretative centre planned. *Drogheda/Slane bus, 4 times daily, 20 mins from Drogheda. Bus Eireann runs day tours from Dublin,* ☎ *8366111.*

Clondalkin. Excellently preserved round tower, from monastery founded as early as the 6th c. CI graveyard opp. has remains of medieval church. In E Clondalkin, some remains of Tully's Castle, built in the 16th c. *51, 51B, 68, 69, 76, 210 buses from city centre to Clondalkin village.*

Coolock. Tumulus topped with trees, in grounds of Cadbury's factory. Ancient burial site was on the route of old Hill of Tara – Wicklow way. Can be seen from public road. *17A, 27, 27A buses from city centre.*

Dunsoghly Castle, *6 km (4 miles) NW of Finglas, E of N2 Dublin – Ashbourne road.* From parapets of 15th c castle, fine views of N Co Dublin, including airport. *Key from nearby cottage; all reasonable times. Dublin – Ashbourne bus from Busaras,*

Dublin; 6 times daily, 30 mins journey.

Glendalough, *51 km (32 miles) S of Dublin.* One of Ireland's most attractive monastic sites. The principal ruins, just E of Lower Lake are the cathedral, with 11th c nave, chancel and St Kevin's Church. 1,000-year-old round tower. St Kevin's Bed, cut into the cliff face S of Upper Lake is less accessible. *Visitor centre open all year, ☎ (0404) 45325/45352. St Kevin's Bus Service operates daily from College of Surgeons, St Stephen's Green, Dublin 2, ☎ 281 8119. Journey time: 1¾ hrs.*

Howth. Large cromlech (prehistoric burial place) in grounds of Howth Castle. On summit, site of burial cairn of Queen Eatair, from whom the ancient name of Howth is said to be derived. *31, 31B buses to Howth village from city centre, (31B to summit),* DART *to Howth.*

Kilmashogue, *Co Dublin, 5.5 km (3.5 miles) S of Rathfarnham on Rockbrook Rd.* Megalithic grave gallery in picturesque glen giving fine views over Dublin. May mark the grave of Irish notables killed in the Battle of Cill Mosamhog, AD 919.

Kilternan, *Co Dublin.* Just past the abbey, an impressive late Stone Age dolmen with large capstone. Sometimes called the Druid's Altar, set under the shadow of Two Rock Mountain. *44 bus from city centre to Kilternan.*

Lusk, *Co Dublin.* Heritage Centre (*see* MUSEUMS).

Mount Venus, *5 km (3 miles) SW of Rathfarnham on Glencree Rd.* Huge prehistoric tablestone, 6 m (20 ft) long. *47, 47A, 47B buses from city centre to Ballyboden.*

Saggart, *Co Dublin.* Graveyard has granite slab and carved cross, all that remains of ancient monastery. 1 km (0.5 mile) SE of village are Adam and Eve stones, which may have prehistoric significance. *69 bus from city centre to Saggart village.*

St Doulagh's Church, *3 km (2 miles) W of Portmarnock.* Parts date back to the 12th c, also subterranean chamber called St Catherine's Well. *Summer, Sat, Sun, 42 bus to Balgriffin.*

Swords, *Co Dublin.* Outer walls of 13th c castle, once a palace of the Archbishop of Dublin. ☎ *840 1291.* Also ancient round tower 22 m (75 ft) high, in good state of preservation. Relic of early

Christian Ireland. *33, 41, 41B, 230 buses every 20 mins from Eden Quay, Dublin, journey time: 50 mins.*
Tibradden, *Co Dublin*: Early Bronze Age burial cairn. *47 bus from city centre to Tibradden.*

ART GALLERIES

In the years immediately following World War II, Dublin's selection of art galleries was very limited: two publicly owned, and an innovative private gallery (Waddington's). Otherwise, art existed in a virtual desert. Today the scene has changed beyond recognition, with numerous smaller galleries nearly all specialising in contemporary local work. The major publicly owned galleries are the National Gallery of Ireland and the Hugh Lane Municipal Gallery. Otherwise, the galleries with the most significant showings are the Douglas Hyde and Kerlin galleries.

Arnotts, *Henry St, Dublin 1,* ☎ *872 1111.* Large department store has frequent art and other exhibitions in top floor gallery. Café. *Mon – Sat.*

Bank of Ireland Arts Centre, *Foster Place, Dublin 2,* ☎ *671 1671.* Art exhibitions, *Mon – Fri, 10 a.m. – 5 p.m.*

Tom Caldwell Gallery, *31 Upper Fitzwilliam St, Dublin 2,* ☎ *668 8269. Tues – Fri, 11 a.m. – 5 p.m., Sat, 11 a.m. – 1 p.m.*

City Arts Centre, *Moss St, Dublin 2,* ☎ *677 0643.* Contemporary art. *Mon – Sat, 11 a.m. – 5.30 p.m.*

Combridge Fine Arts Gallery, *24 Suffolk St, Dublin 2,* ☎ *677 4652.* Regular art showings. *Mon – Sat, 9.30 a.m. – 5.30 p.m.*

Davis Gallery, *11 Capel St, Dublin 1,* ☎ *872 6969.* Gallery artists. *Mon. – Fri. 10 a.m. – 5 p.m., Sat, 11 a.m. – 5 p.m.*

Douglas Hyde Gallery, *Trinity College, Dublin 2, (Nassau St entrance),* ☎ *677 2941 extn 1116.* Shows by leading contemporary Irish and international artists. *Mon – Fri, 11 a.m. – 6 p.m. (Thurs 7 p.m.), Sat, 11 a.m. – 4.45 p.m.*

European Modern Art, *5 Clare St, Dublin 2,* ☎ *676 5371.* 18th c, 19th c works. *Mon – Fri, 10.30 a.m. – 5.30 p.m., Sat, 10.30 a.m. – 1.30 p.m.*

Gallery of Photography, *33-34 East Essex St, Dublin 2,* ☎ *671 4654.* Regular shows of work by leading Irish and international photographers. Modern and historic prints for sale. *Mon−Sat, 11 a.m.−6 p.m., Sun, 12 noon−6 p.m.*

Guinness Hop Store, *Crane St (off Thomas St), Dublin 8,* ☎ *453 6700.* 19th c hop store on four levels converted into an exciting venue for contemporary art. Free Guinness on the ground floor. *Mon−Sat, 10 a.m.−5.30 p.m., Sun, 2.30 p.m.− 5.30 p.m., 21A, 78A, 123 buses.*

Hugh Lane Municipal Gallery of Modern Art, *Parnell Sq, Dublin 1,* ☎ *874 1903.* Dublin city's art collection, including impressionist paintings. Exhibitions, music recitals, poetry readings, lectures. Book shop, restaurant. *Tues−Fri, 9.30 a.m.− 6 p.m., Sat, 9.30 a.m.−5 p.m., Sun, 11 a.m.−5 p.m. Cross-city buses from O'Connell St.*

Kennedy's, *12 Harcourt St, Dublin 2,* ☎ *475 1749.* Contemporary Irish art, mostly by Dublin artists. *Mon−Sat, 10 a.m.−5 p.m.*

Kerlin Gallery, *Annes Lane, off South Anne St, Dublin 2,* ☎ *677 9179.* Outstanding venue for work by leading contemporary artists. *Mon−Fri, 10 a.m.−5.45 p.m., Sat, 11 a.m.−4.30 p.m.*

Bernadette Madden Fabric Studio, *Haddington Rd, Dublin 4,* ☎ *668 6874.* Batik and other textile exhibitions. *By arr. 5, 7, 8, 45 buses from city centre to Haddington Rd.*

Merrion Sq, St Stephen's Green, *Dublin 2.* Open air art exhibitions most weekends in summer.

National College of Art & Design, *Thomas St, Dublin 8,* ☎ *671 1377.* Occasional shows of students' work. *21A, 78A, 123 buses.*

National Concert Hall, *Earlsfort Terrace, Dublin 2,* ☎ *671 1888.* Paintings and other works of art on musical themes. *Daily.*

National Gallery of Ireland, *Merrion Sq West, Dublin 2,* ☎ *661 5133.* Some 2,000 works from all major European schools. World-famous paintings include works by Gainsborough, Goya and Poussin. *The Taking of Christ* by Caravaggio is especially worth seeing. Irish artists include Hone, Lavery, Osborne, Jack B. Yeats. Regular annual exhibitions include Turner watercolours (*Jan, Feb*) and visiting international shows. Full educational programme. Restaurant. *Mon−Sat, 10 a.m.−5.15 p.m. (Thurs, 8 p.m.), Sun, 2 p.m.−5 p.m.*

National Library, *Kildare St, Dublin 2,* ☎ *661 8811.* Frequent photographic and art exhibitions, *Mon−Sat, (see* LIBRARIES*).*

Neptune Gallery, *41 South William St, Dublin 2,* ☎ *671 5021. Engravings, paintings and prints from 18th c, 19th c. Mon−Fri, 10 a.m.−6 p.m., Sat, 10 a.m.−1 p.m.*

Oisin Gallery, *10 Marino Mart, Dublin 3,* ☎ *833 3456.* Contemporary Irish art. *Mon−Fri, 9 a.m.−5.30 p.m., Sat, 10 a.m.−5.30 p.m. 20A, 20B, 30, 44A buses.*

Oriel Gallery, *17 Clare St, Dublin 2,* ☎ *676 3410.* Regular exhibitions, including works by Markey Robinson, Percy French, Jack B. Yeats. *Mon−Fri, 10 a.m.−5.30 p.m., Sat, 10 a.m.−1 p.m.*

Peacock Theatre (foyer), *Lr Abbey St, Dublin 1,* ☎ *878 7222.* Regular exhibitions.

Project Arts Centre, *East Essex St, Temple Bar, Dublin 2,* ☎ *671 2321.* Good venue for shows of contemporary, often avant garde work. *Mon−Sat, 11 a.m.−6 p.m.*

RHA Gallagher Gallery, *Ely Place, Dublin 2,* ☎ *661 2558.* Outstanding and very spacious modern venue for contemporary shows. *Mon−Sat, 11 a.m.−5 p.m. (Thurs, 9 p.m.), Sun, 2 p.m.−5 p.m.*

Solomon Gallery, *Powerscourt Townhouse Centre, Dublin 2,* ☎ *679 4237.* Regular shows of contemporary art, including paintings, sculptures. *Mon−Sat, 10 a.m.−5.30 p.m., Sun, 12 noon−5.30 p.m.*

Taylor Galleries, *34 Kildare St, Dublin 2,* ☎ *676 6055.* Contemporary art. *Mon−Fri, 10 a.m.−5.30 p.m., Sat, 11 a.m.−1 p.m.*

United Arts Club, *3 Upper Fitzwilliam St, Dublin 2,* ☎ *676 2965.* Shows of members' work.

BLUE PLAQUES

Dublin has been host to an extraordinary number of extremely talented people through the years, not just in literature, but in other branches of the arts and sciences. Blue plaques mark the birth-places, and in some cases the residences, of famous Dublin people, as well as outsiders who settled in the city. Most of the recorded hereunder have their birthplaces, and/or their residences, marked by blue plaques. In a small number of cases a building may not have an inscription on it as yet, but the following entries will form a fascinating history trail through the city.

Kevin Barry, young Volunteer who was executed at age of 18 in 1920 by British forces. Born at 8 Fleet St, Dublin 2, (opp. ESB showrooms).

Samuel Beckett, poet, playwright. Cooldrinagh, Foxrock village, Dublin 18, was his birthplace, 1906. *63, 86 buses from city centre to Foxrock.*

Brendan Behan, playwright. His birthplace at Russell St, off Mountjoy Sq, is now demolished. For many of the later years of his life, he lived at 5 Anglesea Rd, Ballsbridge, Dublin 4. *5, 7, 8, 45 bus to RDS. Also* DART *to Lansdowne Rd, 500 metres.*

Bewley's, *Grafton St.* Blue plaque on front notes that during the 18th c, Samuel Whyte's school stood on this site. Pupils included Robert Emmet, Thomas Moore, Richard Sheridan and the Duke of Wellington. Small museum now on premises.

Elizabeth Bowen, novelist. Born in 1899 at 15 Herbert Place, off Lower Baggot St, Dublin 2.

Isaac Butt, great 19th c patriot and parliamentarian. Died in house at corner of Clonskeagh Rd and Wynnsward Drive, Clonskeagh, 5 May 1879. Plaque on exterior wall. *11, 62 buses from city centre to Clonskeagh Rd.*

Edward Carson, 'architect' of Northern Ireland. Born at 4 Harcourt St, Dublin 2, in 1854. Later went to Trinity College, Dublin.

Sir Roger Casement, British diplomat, Irish patriot, executed in 1916. Born at 29 Lawson Terrace, Sandycove Rd, 1864. *8 bus* *from city centre to Sandycove Rd.* DART *to Sandycove, 700 metres.*

Michael Davitt, founder of Land League, a pivotal political force in late 19th c Ireland. Lived for many years at Land League cottage, Military Rd, Ballybrack, Co Dublin. DART *to Killiney, 500 metres.*

John Dunlop, inventor of pneumatic tyre. Lived at 46 Ailesbury Rd, Donnybrook, Dublin 4 (now the Belgian Embassy residence). Dunlop tyres were first made at 67 Upper Stephen St, Dublin 2. *5, 7, 8, 45 buses to Merrion Rd.*

John Field, composer and pianist. Golden Lane, Dublin 8 (off Whitefriar St). Born here, 1782. Invented the nocturne (later exploited by Chopin) and won fame in Moscow.

Barry Fitzgerald, Irish actor, Hollywood film star. Born in 1888, 1 Walworth Rd, Portobello, Dublin 8. Later lived at 50 Sandymount Ave, until he moved to Hollywood. *16, 19, 22A buses to South Circular Rd for Walworth Rd.* DART *to Sandymount for Sandymount Ave, 300 metres.*

Bob Geldof, rock musician, Third World fund-raiser. Educated at Blackrock College, Booterstown, Co Dublin. Later, he commented on his time there in mostly unfavourable terms. *5, 7, 8, 45 buses to Booterstown.* DART *to Booterstown, 300 metres.*

Oliver St John Gogarty, Dublin surgeon/writer with cutting wit. From 1915 to 1917 he had rooms in the Shelbourne Hotel. His house at nearby 5 Upper Ely Place has since been demolished.

Maude Gonne, famed Irish nationalist, great influence on W .B. Yeats. Roebuck House, Clonskeagh Rd, Dublin 14 was her home for just over 30 years, until her death in 1953. Her son, Sean MacBride, also lived here for many years until his death in 1988. *11, 62 buses from city centre.*

George Friedrich Handel, composer of the *Messiah*. Written at a house in Middle Abbey St (city centre), it was first performed in 1742 at the new Musick Hall in Fishamble St (near City Hall). Neither building exists today, although the streets still remain.

Rex Ingram, noted pioneering Hollywood film director. Born in 1892 at 58 Grosvenor Sq, Rathmines, Dublin 6. *47, 47B buses* *from city centre to Leinster Rd.*

James Joyce, novelist. Born in 1882 at 41 Brighton Sq, Rathgar, Dublin 6. Brighton Square is not a square, but a green-centred triangle. Joyce spent the first 22 years of his life in Dublin and lived at 23 addresses. *16, 16A, 49, 49A, 65 buses from city centre to Harold's Cross Rd/Terenure Rd N. 5 mins walk.*

Patrick Kavanagh, poet. He lived at 62 Pembroke Rd, and also at 19 Raglan Rd, in 1958–59. He died in 1967. *5, 7, 8, 45 buses from city centre to US Embassy.*

Micheál MacLiammóir, one of Ireland's greatest actors, lived at 4 Harcourt Terrace, Adelaide Rd, Dublin 2, until his death in 1978. He shared the house with another great theatrical personality, the late Hilton Edwards. *14, 15A, 15B, 44, 47, 48A, 62 buses to Adelaide Rd.*

Dr John Mahaffy, the most colourful occupant of the Provost's House, Trinity College. Professor of Greek in the time of Joyce and Wilde.

Guglielmo Marconi, wireless telegraphy inventor. Related by marriage to the Jameson distillery family who owned Montrose house, now part of the RTE complex at Donnybrook. *10, 46A buses from city centre to RTE.*

John McCormack, world-famous singer. Died in 1945 at Glena, Rock Rd, Booterstown, Co Dublin (main road to Dun Laoghaire). Plaque on house front records fact. *5, 7, 8, 45 buses from city centre to Rock Rd. DART to Booterstown, 400 metres.*

W. H. S. Monck, 16 Earlsfort Terrace, Dublin 2: first electrical measurement of starlight took place here, 1892.

Thomas Moore, poet, songwriter. 12 Aungier St, Dublin 2 was his birthplace, 1779. Now a pub. *5 mins walk from St Stephen's Green W.*

T. C. Murray, early 20th c playwright. Closely associated with Abbey Theatre, lived at 11 Sandymount Ave, Dublin 4. DART to Sandymount, *5, 7, 8, 45 buses from city centre to Merrion Rd.*

Lord Northcliffe, pioneer of British newspaper industry, founder of *Daily Mail*. Born in 1865 at Sunnybank, Chapelizod, Dublin 20. *25, 26, 66, 66A, 67, 67A buses from city centre to Chapelizod.*

Daniel O'Connell, leader of Catholic Emancipation. Ireland's Liberator lived at 58 Merrion Sq, Dublin 2 for many years. *City centre buses to Merrion Sq.* DART *to Pearse station, Westland Row, 700 metres.*

Brian O'Nolan, alias Flann O'Brien/Myles na gCopaleen, the great Irish humorous writer. Lived at Avoca Rd (off Avoca Ave), Blackrock, Co Dublin. Plaque on house front records his residence. *5, 7, 8 buses, or* DART, *to Blackrock. Walk up Carysfort Ave to Avoca Ave.*

George Russell (AE), philosopher, poet, writer. Worked at 84 Merrion Sq. *All city centre buses to Merrion Sq.* Lived for many years at 17 Rathgar Ave. *15A bus to Rathgar crossroads.*

Cornelius Ryan, chronicler of World War II. Born in 1920 at 33 Heytesbury St, off South Circular Rd, Dublin 8. *16, 16A, 19, 19A, 22A buses to South Circular Rd (Harrington St).*

Erwin Schroedinger. The creator of wave mechanisms, worked at 65 Merrion Sq, Dublin 2 between 1940 and 1956 and lived at 26 Kincora Rd, Clontarf, Dublin 3.

George Bernard Shaw, playwright and critic. Born 1856 at 33 Synge St, off Harrington St, South Circular Rd, Dublin 8. As a boy, he lived at Shaw's Cottage, otherwise Torca Cottage, on Dalkey Hill. His Synge St birthplace has been turned into a museum. *16, 16A, 19, 19A, 22A, 55 buses from city centre to Harrington St. 8 bus,* DART *from city centre to Dalkey, 800 metres.*

Joseph Sheridan le Fanu, master of the 19th c Gothic horror story. For the last 22 years of his life, lived at 70 Merrion Sq, Dublin 2.

Charles Villiers Stanford, composer. Born at 2 Herbert St in 1852.

Bram Stoker, author of *Dracula*. Born at 15 Marino Crescent, Clontarf, Dublin 3 in 1847. Later lived at 16 Harcourt St. *24, 51A, 123 buses to Marino.*

Anthony Trollope, Victorian novelist. Although English, he spent some 16 years in Ireland, working for the post office. For five of those years, he lived at 6 Seaview Terrace, off Ailesbury Rd,

Donnybrook, Dublin 4. *10, 46A buses from city centre to Donnybrook Church, then 5 mins walk.* DART *to Sydney Parade station, 800 metres.*

Oscar Wilde, playwright, wit. Born 1854 at 21 Westland Row, Dublin 2. One year later, moved to 1 Merrion Sq, Dublin 2.

Ludwig Wittgenstein, Austrian philosopher. Spent two years in Dublin (1947—49). Wrote his greatest works in what was then Rosses Hotel. Now Ashling Hotel, beside Heuston station.

Jack B. Yeats, painter. Lived at 18 Fitzwilliam Sq (corner of Fitzwilliam Place), Dublin 2.

W. B. Yeats, poet. Born in 1865 at 5 Sandymount Ave, Dublin 4. Later lived at 52 and 82 Merrion Sq, Dublin 2. In the latter house, which he bought in 1922, he held stately Monday evening 'at homes'. According to Gogarty, this was Yeats's 'silk hat period'. DART *to Sandymount, 400 metres to Sandymount Ave.*

CHURCHES

Dublin has a host of churches of all denominations. Most Catholic churches are of 19th c origin, built following Catholic Emancipation in 1829. Generally, 20th c church building in Dublin has been uninspiring. Many Protestant, particularly Church of Ireland churches, have far older antecedents. While Catholic churches are normally freely open during the day, Protestant churches are usually kept closed apart from times of services. Noticeboards give the telephone number of church officers for further information. Dublin also has two Church of Ireland cathedrals, but only one Catholic Pro-Cathedral. c denotes Roman Catholic, CI Church of Ireland.

Abbey Presbyterian Church, *Parnell Sq (next to Writer's Museum).* Opened 1864, its construction funded by noted Dublin grocer, Alex Findlater. *Summer, Mon—Sat, 10 a.m. —2 p.m.*

Christ Church Cathedral (CI), *Christchurch Place, Dublin 2.* Founded 1038, rebuilt by the Normans following their invasion in 1169. Magnificent stonework on nave and aisles. See alleged tomb of Strongbow. Extensive, but dusty, crypt, dates from Norman times. *Daily, 10 a.m. – 5 p.m.*

Church of Sacred Heart (C), *Donnybrook, Dublin 4*. Built in 1863. Edward, son of the great architect Augustus Pugin, was deeply involved in its English-style design. A pleasing and homely interior. *10, 46A buses from city centre to Donnybrook.*

Delgany Parish Church (CI), *Co Wicklow*. Attractive building dating back to 1789. Construction funded by Peter La Touche, a member of the Huguenot family, instrumental in development of banking in Dublin. Church has many interesting plaques, also extravagant memorial to David La Touche. Splendid views of surrounding wooded countryside from graveyard. *84 bus every hour from College St, Dublin 2, or* DART *to Bray, then 84A bus. Journey time: 1½ hrs.*

Our Lady of Lourdes Church (C), *Sean MacDermott St*. Tomb of Matt Talbot, early 20th c dock worker, a saintly and ascetic figure much venerated in the Catholic church.

Pro-Cathedral (C), *Marlborough St, off O'Connell St*. Built in early 19th c in Grecian-Doric style. Interior is very similar to that of St Phillipe du Roule, Paris. Fascinating, but ghoulish, crypt is now open to brave-hearted visitors.

Rotunda Hospital Chapel, *Parnell Sq, Dublin 1*. Small, early 18th c chapel is full of elaborate rococo plasterwork. Much of the chapel is decorated in biblical themes. *By arr., hospital secretary,* ☎ *873 0700.*

St Andrew's (CI), *Suffolk St, Dublin 2*. The original church dated back to 11th c and was the first outside the city walls. The present church, with its fine spire, was built in 1866. It contains impressively preserved records going back to Restoration times. Esther van Hormrigh, Swift's 'Vanessa', was buried here, but the grave site is unmarked. The building will open in 1995 in its new guise as the main TIO for Dublin city centre.

St Ann's Church (CI), *Dawson St, Dublin 2* . One of Dublin's finest 18th c churches. Plain exterior belies fascinating interior. *Open daily.*

St Audoen's Church (CI), *Cornmarket, Dublin 8*. Oldest parish church in city, dating from late 12th c. Although partially ruined, portion is still used. St Audoen's Arch, dating from 1215, is the only remaining portion of ancient city walls. *Open Sun. 21A, 78A, 123 buses to High St.*

St Augustine and John(C), *Thomas St, Dublin 8*. Large and impressive church designed in the early 1860s in the French Gothic style. Situated in one of the city's most absorbing areas. Adjoining John's Lane has great historical atmosphere. *21A, 78A, 123 buses from city centre.*

St Bartholomew's (CI), *Clyde Rd, Ballsbridge, Dublin 4*. Near to the US Embassy, this 19th c church, built 1865−67, has many fascinating Byzantine interior features, including painted choir, that make it rich and strange by comparison with many of its contemporary churches in Dublin. Similar in style to University Church, St Stephen's Green. *5, 7, 8, 45 buses to US Embassy, then 2 mins walk.*

St Francis Xavier (C), *Upper Gardiner St, Dublin 1*. Many consider it to be the city's finest church. Designed by J. B. Keane, who was also involved in the construction of the Pro-Cathedral, the church was the first built in Dublin after Catholic Emancipation in 1829. It opened in 1832; the building is in the shape of a Latin cross. The marble of the high altar came from Rome, some from Nero's Golden House. *3, 11, 16, 40, 40A, 41, 41A, 41C buses from city centre to Upper Gardiner St.*

St George's Church (CI), *Hardwicke Place, Temple St, Dublin 1*. With its high spire, the building, completed in 1814, is modelled on St Martin-in-the-Fields, London. Fine decorated ceiling.

St John's Church (CI), *St John's Rd, Sandymount, Dublin 4*. Built in 1850 and said to be replica of a church in Normandy. Caen stone used in its construction. *June−Aug, Sat, Sun, Wed, 2 p.m. − 5.30 p.m. 3 bus to Church.*

St Joseph's Church (CI), *Berkeley St, Dublin 7*. Victorian church opened in 1880. Adjacent is 1876 memorial to the four 17c chroniclers who wrote the great classic of ancient Irish history, the *Annals of the Four Masters. 10, 19, 19A, 22, 38, 120 buses from city centre to Doyle's Corner, Phibsboro', then 5 mins walk.*

St Michan's Church (CI), *Church St, Dublin 7.* 17th c church famous for preserved bodies in the vaults. Dry atmosphere has helped to keep them in pristine condition. Handel is said to have played the organ here. *Mon−Fri, 10 a.m. −12.45 p.m.; 2 p.m. − 4.45 p.m. Sat, 10 a.m. −12.45 p.m. Mornings only, Mon−Sat. Nov−Mar. ☎ 872 4154. At other times, caretaker in adjacent Castle St has key. 34 bus from city centre to Church St.*

St Patrick's Cathedral(CI), *Patrick St, Dublin 8.* Founded 1190, restored about 1860. Jonathan Swift was Dean from 1713 to 1745, his tomb is in the South aisle 'where savage indignation can no longer render his heart'. See also monument to Turlough O'Carolan, last of the Irish bards. Daily all year. 50, 50A, 54, 54A, 56A buses.

St Stephen (CI), *Upper Mount St, Dublin 2.* Present church, with its fine entrance columns and pepper pot cupola, was built in 1824. Previous church of this name was on site of Mercer's hospital in Stephen St; that church dated back to at least 1244. The interior of the present church has interesting galleries on three sides; nevertheless, the exterior is more imposing than the interior.

St Theresa's Church (C), *Clarendon St, off Grafton St, Dublin 2.* Building began in 1793 when penal laws against Catholics in Ireland were still in force, hence deceptively low-key exterior and entrance. Plaque details church history. *Open daily.*

Trinity College Chapel. Completed in 1798, with wooden stalls, panelling and ceiling stucco work of period. Casework on organ restored to original George III era splendour.

University Church (CI), *St Stephen's Green, Dublin 2.* With its Byzantine-style interior, this church is one of Cardinal Newman's finest legacies to Dublin. Built between 1855 and 1856, the church has many unusual design features, including wall decorations and carvings. Its architect was John Hungerford Pollen.

Whitefriars St Church (C), *Dublin 8.* St Valentine, patron saint of lovers, is buried beneath the altar. His remains were brought here from Rome in 1836. Church stands on site of pre-Reformation Dublin Priory, which was destroyed in 1539. Present church was opened in 1827, two years before Catholic Emancipation, but only left-hand aisle. Rest of church wasn't completed until end of the 19th c. ☎ *475 8821.*

CHURCH SERVICES
The majority religion is Roman Catholic and all churches have services on Sundays and daily throughout the week. Protestant churches tend to confine services to Sundays. Many other denominations have established churches in the city in recent years; you can even attend a German Lutheran or Greek Orthodox service if you wish. Several other faiths, such as Islam, are now represented. For full details of church services and times, contact local TIO.

Roman Catholic. Sunday Masses usually take place in mornings and early evenings, between 8 a.m. and 1 p.m. and between 5 p.m. and 7 p.m. For details of Masses in Latin ☎ *284 2206.* Of special interest is the Mass in Latin at the Pro-Cathedral, every Sunday, 11 a.m., sung by Palestrina Choir. Otherwise, Masses are celebrated daily. Check individual church notices for details.

Church of Ireland. Eucharist and Matins are held on Sunday mornings, while Evensong is held every Sunday between 3 p.m. and 7 p.m. With the exception of the cathedrals, few services take place during the rest of the week.

Presbyterian. Sunday services are held at the Abbey Church, Parnell Sq, Adelaide Rd, Christ Church, Rathgar, Christ Church, Sandymount, Clontarf, York Rd, Dun Laoghaire, Howth and Malahide. Sunday mornings and evenings, the latter at 7 p.m.

Methodist. Services are held on Sunday mornings and evenings (11.30 a.m. and 7 p.m.) at Centenary Church, Leeson Park, Christ Church, Sandymount, Drimnagh, Dundrum, Rathgar, Clontarf, Skerries, Sutton.

Baptist. Grosvenor Baptist Church, Grosvenor Rd, Rathmines, Dublin 6. Sunday, 11 a.m., 7 p.m.

Christian Science. First Church: 21 Herbert Park, Dublin 4. Sunday, 11 a.m., Wednesday, 8 p.m.

Lutheran. St Finian's, Adelaide Rd, Dublin 2. Sunday, 11 a.m. (service in German).

Quakers. Pakenham Rd, Monkstown, Co Dublin; 62 Crannagh Rd, Rathfarnham, Dublin 14. ☎ *668 3684 for information.*

Seventh Day Adventists. 47A Ranelagh Rd, Dublin 6. Services on Wednesday, Saturday, Sunday.

Greek Orthodox. The Annunciation and St Andrew, Mount Pleasant, Ranelagh Rd, Dublin 6. Sunday, 11 a.m.

Jewish. *Orthodox*: 27 Adelaide Rd, Dublin 2; Greenville Hall synagogue, Dolphin's Barn, Dublin 8; Rathfarnham Rd synagogue, Dublin 6. Saturday, 9.15 a.m. *Progressive*: 7 Leicester Ave, Rathgar, Dublin 6. Friday p.m., Saturday a.m.

Islam. Dublin Islamic Centre, South Circular Rd, Dublin 8 (next to National Stadium), ☎ *453 3242. Friday—Juma prayers, also daily prayers.*

EMBASSIES

Argentina. *15 Ailesbury Drive, Dublin 4,* ☎ *269 1546/269 4603.*

Australia. *6th floor, Fitzwilton House, Wilton Tce, Dublin 2,* ☎ *676 1517.*

Austria. *15 Ailesbury Court, 93 Ailesbury Rd, Dublin 4,* ☎ *269 4577/269 1451.*

Belgium. *2 Shrewsbury Rd, Dublin 4,* ☎ *269 2082/269 1588.*

Canada. *4th floor, 65-68 St Stephen's Green, Dublin 2,* ☎ *478 1988.*

China. *40 Ailesbury Rd, Dublin 4,* ☎ *269 1707.*

Denmark. *121—122 St Stephen's Green, Dublin 2,* ☎ *475 6404/475 6405.*

Egypt. *12 Clyde Rd, Dublin 4,* ☎ *660 6566/660 6718.*

Finland. *Stokes Place, St Stephen's Green, Dublin 2,* ☎ *478 1344.*

France. *36 Ailesbury Rd, Dublin 4,* ☎ *269 4777.*

Germany. *1 Trimleston Ave, Booterstown, Co Dublin,* ☎ *269 3011.*

Greece. *1 Upper Pembroke St, Dublin 2,* ☎ *676 7254/676 7255.*

Holy See. *183 Navan Rd, Dublin 7,* ☎ *838 0577.*

Hungary. *2 Fitzwilliam Place, Dublin 2,* ☎ *661 2902.*

India. *6 Leeson Pk, Dublin 6,* ☎ *497 0843/497 0959.*
Iran. *72 Mount Merrion Ave, Blackrock, Co Dublin,* ☎ *288 0252.*
Italy. *63-65 Northumberland Rd, Dublin 4,* ☎ *660 1744.*
Japan. *Merrion Centre, Dublin 4,* ☎ *269 4244/269 4033.*
Korea. *20 Clyde Rd, Dublin 4,* ☎ *660 8800.*
Netherlands. *160 Merrion Rd, Dublin 4,* ☎ *269 3444.*
Nigeria. *56 Leeson Pk, Dublin 6,* ☎ *660 4366/660 4051.*
Norway. *34 Molesworth St, Dublin 2,* ☎ *662 1800.*
Portugal. *Knocksinna House, Knocksinna Rd, Foxrock, Co Dublin,* ☎ *289 4416.*
Russian Federation. *186 Orwell Road, Dublin 14,* ☎ *492 3525.*
Spain. *17A Merlyn Park, Dublin 4,* ☎ *269 1649/269 2597.*
Sweden. *Sun Alliance House, 13–17 Dawson St, Dublin 2,* ☎ *671 5822.*
Switzerland. *6 Ailesbury Rd, Dublin 4,* ☎ *269 2515.*
Turkey. *60 Merrion Rd, Dublin 4,* ☎ *668 5240/660 1623.*
UK. *Merrion Rd, Dublin 4,* ☎ *269 5211.*
USA. *42 Elgin Rd, Dublin 4,* ☎ *668 8777.*

ENTERTAINMENT

CABARET
The cabaret scene is lively, with the Burlington and Jury's hotels serving rousing singing and dancing, unashamedly aimed at American audiences. Clontarf Castle, on Dublin's northside, has developed into a good entertainment venue. For really traditional Irish entertainment, in the old style, without being folksy, try Comhaltas Ceoltóirí Éireann at Monkstown. Dublin does not have the erotic or satirical cabarets of continental cities, such as Berlin and Paris.
Abbey Tavern, *Howth, Co Dublin,* ☎ *839 0307.*
Burlington Hotel, *Upper Leeson St, Dublin 4,* ☎ *660 5222.*
Clontarf Castle, *Castle Ave, Dublin 3,* ☎ *833 2271.*
Comhaltas Ceoltóirí Éireann, *32 Belgrave Sq, Monkstown, Co Dublin,* ☎ *280 0295.* Traditional Irish music cabaret.

Green Isle Hotel, *Naas Rd, Clondalkin, Dublin 22,* ☎ *459 3406.*
Jury's Hotel, *Ballsbridge, Dublin 4,* ☎ *660 5000.*

CINEMAS

Cinemas still thrive in Dublin, particularly in the city centre, though, with a few honourable exceptions, suburban cinemas are thin on the ground. In the city centre there are just over 20 screens (some of the cinemas have up to five screens). Programme offerings are not so good, due to problems of film distribution. Popular American films are shown soon after release, but Dublin has a severe shortage of art films with few venues for showing them. However, the Screen, D'Olier St makes some forays in this direction and the Lighthouse in Middle Abbey St complements the Irish Film Centre in showing this type of film.

Adelphi, *Middle Abbey St, Dublin 1,* ☎ *873 1161.* 4 screens.
Ambassador, *Parnell Sq, Dublin 1 (top of O'Connell St),* ☎ *872 7000.*
Classic, *Harold's Cross Rd, Dublin 6,* ☎ *492 3324.* 2 screens.
Forum, *Glasthule Rd, Dun Laoghaire, Co Dublin,* ☎ *280 9574.* 2 screens. DART *to Sandycove.*
Irish Film Centre, *Eustace St (off Dame St), Dublin 2,* ☎ *679 3477.* 2 screens, national film archives, bar, restaurant.
Lighthouse, *Middle Abbey St, Dublin 1,* ☎ *873 0438.*
Ormonde, *Stillorgan Plaza, Co Dublin,* ☎ *283 1144.* 3 screens.
Royal Cineplex, *Quinsboro Rd, Bray,* ☎ *286 8686.*
Santry Omniplex, *Dublin 9,* ☎ *842 8844.* 10 screens.
Savoy, *Upper O'Connell St, Dublin 1,* ☎ *874 6000.* 5 screens.
Screen, *D'Olier St, Dublin 2,* ☎ *671 4988.* 3 screens.
Stella, *Rathmines Rd, Rathmines, Dublin 6,* ☎ *497 1281.* 2 screens.
UCI, *Malahide Rd, Coolock, Dublin 17,* ☎ *848 5122.* 10 screens.

CLASSICAL MUSIC

For classical music, there is only one major venue in Dublin, the National Concert Hall in Earlsfort Terrace. In its main auditorium there is a constant variety of musical entertainment throughout the year, often featuring some of the world's top orchestras. The hall is frequently used to stage middle-of-the-road entertainment, again featuring world-class entertainers. The smaller recital hall at the NCH has interesting programmes throughout the year. Besides the NCH other venues do offer classical music from time to time, such as Trinity College and the Royal Hospital, Kilmainham. Some of the city-centre and suburban churches occasionally offer musical events, such as organ recitals. The daily newspapers, particulary *The Irish Times*, have good listings of these events.

National Concert Hall, *Earlsfort Terrace, Dublin 2,* ☎ *671 1888.* Credit card bookings, ☎ *671 1533.* Daily musical events, all year. Larger scale performances in main hall, recitals in John Field Room. Bar and catering.

DISCOS AND NIGHTCLUBS

Predicting which of these venues is likely to be 'in' or even still open in 12 months' time is like trying to produce long-range weather forecasts. There is nothing outrageous about any of the discos and nightclubs in Dublin, except the price of wine in certain establishments. Well-established discos are to be found in some hotels, such as the Gresham, Sachs and Sands (Portmarnock). Discos and nightclubs are no longer centred around Lower Leeson St, but much more widely spread through the city. Licensing regulations tend to be flexible so that, if you wish, you can drink until dawn. Most discos charge an entrance fee of about £5, while nightclubs often admit you for nothing, then charge high prices for the drinks. A mediocre bottle of wine can cost £15, while for champagne, the sky's the limit.

Annabel's, *Burlington Hotel, Dublin 4,* ☎ *660 5222.*

Buck Whaleys, *67 Lr Leeson St, Dublin 2,* ☎ *676 1755.*

Chiki's, *Harcourt Hotel, Harcourt St, Dublin 2,* ☎ *478 3677.*

Club M, *Blooms Hotel, Anglesea St, Dublin 2,* ☎ *679 0277.*

Club Paradiso, *Irish Film Centre, Eustace St, Dublin 2,* ☎ *677 8788.*

Cocos, *Belgard Complex, Tallaght, Dublin 24,* ☎ *451 3132.*

Faces, *Braemor Rd, Churchtown, Dublin 14,* ☎ *296 0099.*

Gigis, *Russell Court Hotel, Harcourt St, Dublin 2,* ☎ *478 4066.*
Howl at the Moon, *8 Lr Mount St, Dublin 2,* ☎ *676 1717.*
The Kitchen, *Clarence Hotel, Wellington Quay, Dublin 2,* ☎ *677 6178.*
Leggs, *29 Lr Leeson St, Dublin 2,* ☎ *676 6269.*
Lillies Bordello, *Adam Court, Grafton St, Dublin 2,* ☎ *679 9204.*
The Loft, *Purty Kitchen, Old Dunleary Rd, Dun Laoghaire, Co Dublin,* ☎ *284 3576.*
Peg Woffington's City Club, *Kildare St, Dublin 2,* ☎ *679 4380.*
Pink Elephant, *Setanta Centre, South Frederick St, Dublin 2,* ☎ *677 5876.*
Raffles, *Sachs Hotel, Morehampton Rd, Donnybrook, Dublin 4,* ☎ *668 4829.*
Rumours, *19 Upper O'Connell St, Dublin 1,* ☎ *872 3936.*
Strings, *24 Lr Leeson St, Dublin 2,* ☎ *661 3664.*
Tamango's, *Sands Hotel, Portmarnock, Co Dublin,* ☎ *846 0003.*
Temple of Sound, *Ormond Hotel, Upper Ormond Quay, Dublin 7,* ☎ *872 1811.*
The Pod, *35 Harcourt St, Dublin 2,* ☎ *478 0166.*
Zoe's, *5 Wicklow St, Dublin 2,* ☎ *679 7530.*

MUSIC VENUES

In recent years, Dublin has spawned an amazing selection of music venues. As with other entertainment places, fashions change fast and this year's 'in' places can be decidedly 'out' by next year. But some venues continue in full bloom for years. For traditional ballads with a strongly entertainment-slanted treatment, try the Abbey Tavern in Howth, but if you prefer a more traditional purist approach, try some of the established pub venues, such as An Béal Bocht or O'Donoghues. The many other pub venues listed are fairly reliable, but you would be advised to check in advance as the entertainment offered may vary from time to time. In this listing the following abbreviations have been used: **B** (ballad singing), **C** (country music), **F** (folk music), **J** (jazz), **R** (rock), **T** (traditional).
Abbey Tavern, *Howth, Co Dublin,* ☎ *839 0307.* **B, T**

An Beál Bocht, *Charlemont St, Dublin 2,* ☎ *475 5614.* **F, T**

Bad Bob's Backstage Bar, *34 East Essex St, Dublin 2,* ☎ *677 5482.* **C**

Baggot Inn, *143 Lower Baggot St, Dublin 2,* ☎ *676 1430.* **R**

Barge Inn, *42 Charlemont St, Dublin 2,* ☎ *475 0005.* **J**

Barry's Hotel, *1-2 Great Denmark St, Dublin 1,* ☎ *874 6943.* **C**

Boss Croker's, *39 Arran Quay, Dublin 7,* ☎ *872 2400.* **F, J, R, T**

Brazen Head, *20 Lower Bridge St, Dublin 8,* ☎ *679 9549.* **F, J, T**

Bruxelles, *Harry St, off Grafton St, Dublin 2,* ☎ *677 8731.* **J**

Castle Inn, *5 Lord Edward St, Dublin 2,* ☎ *478 3756.* **R**

Central Hotel, *Exchequer St, Dublin 2,* ☎ *679 7302.* **T**

Cock Tavern, *18 Church St, Howth,* ☎ *832 3237.* **F, R**

Court Hotel, *Killiney, Co Dublin,* ☎ *285 1622.* **J**

Downeys, *Grange Cross, Ballyfermot, Dublin 10,* ☎ *626 4679.* **F**

Four Seasons, *199 North King St, Dublin 1,* ☎ *872 1770.* **F**

Foxes, *Glencullen, Co Dublin,* ☎ *295 5647.* **B, F**

Grattan, *Capel St, Dublin 1,* ☎ *873 3049.* **J**

Ha'penny Bridge Inn, *42 Wellington Quay, Dublin 2,* ☎ *677 0416.* **F, T**

Harcourt Hotel, *Harcourt St, Dublin 2,* ☎ *878 3677.* **J**

Hotel Pierre, *Dun Laoghaire seafront,* ☎ *280 0291.* **J**

Hughes, *Chancery St, Dublin 7,* ☎ *872 6540.* **F**

International Bar, *Wicklow St, Dublin 2,* ☎ *677 9250.* **·J**

Kennedy's, *Westland Row, Dublin 2,* ☎ *676 2998.* **T**

Lower Deck, *Portobello Harbour, Dublin 8,* ☎ *475 1423.* **B**

McDaid's, *3 Harry St, Dublin 2,* ☎ *679 4395.* **J**

Mother Redcap's, *Back Lane, Dublin 8,* ☎ *453 8306.* **F, T**

National Stadium, *South Circular Rd, Dublin 8,* ☎ *453 3371.* **R**

O'Donoghue's, *Merrion Row, Dublin 2,* ☎ *660 7194.* **T**

Kitty O'Shea's, *23 Upper Grand Canal St, Dublin 4,* ☎ *660 9965.* **B, C, R**

Pembroke Inn, *31 Lower Pembroke St, Dublin 2,* ☎ *660 5767.* **F**

Piper's Club, *Henrietta St, Dublin 7,* ☎ *874 4447.* **F,T**

Point Theatre, *East Link Bridge, Dublin 1,* ☎ *836 6777.* **F, R**

Purty Loft, *Old Dunleary Rd, Dun Laoghaire, Co Dublin,* ☎ *280 1257.* **F, B, J, R**
Red Cow, *Naas Rd, Clondalkin, Dublin 22,* ☎ *459 1250.* **F, T**
Ryans, *Queen St, Dublin 7,* ☎ *872 5061.* **F, T**
Sachs Hotel, *Morehampton Rd, Dublin 4,* ☎ *668 0955.* **J**
Sir Arthur Conan Doyle, *Phibsboro', Dublin 7,* ☎ *830 1441.* **J**
Slatterys, *Capel St, Dublin 1,* ☎ *874 0416.* **F, T**
Waterfront, *Sir John Rogerson's Quay, Dublin 2,* ☎ *679 9258.* **R**
Wexford Inn, *Wexford St, Dublin 2,* ☎ *478 1588.* **B**
Whelan's, *Wexford St, Dublin 2,* ☎ *478 0766.* **R, T**

THEATRES

The amount of theatrical activity in Dublin belies the size of the city. The Abbey Theatre is the national theatre and sometimes suffers from the need to revive old classics, but in recent times it has regained some of its formerly lively reputation. Its smaller, sister theatre, the Peacock, down in the basement, sometimes has good experimental drama, although the best venue for this is the Project. The Olympia is a marvellous example of a 19th c building, well restored, with a broad selection of theatrical and musical entertainment. A similar role is played by the equally well-restored Gaiety Theatre. The Gate, once the theatrical home of Micheál MacLiammoir and Hilton Edwards, has been returned to its former glory, offering the most exciting productions in Dublin.

Abbey, *Lower Abbey St, Dublin 1,* ☎ *878 7222.* Ireland's national theatre has suffered from too safe a reputation in recent years, but there are still some worthwhile productions. Interesting theatrical portraits. The new façade adds architectural interest.
Andrew's Lane, *off St Andrew's St, Dublin 2,* ☎ *679 5720.* Intimate setting for lively, often controversial productions.
City Arts Centre, *23-25 Moss St, Dublin 2,* ☎ *677 0643.* Avant garde theatre.
Eblana, *Busarus, Store St, Dublin 1,* ☎ *867 0007.* Occasional performances in small theatre in basement of bus station.
Focus, *Pembroke Place (off Pembroke St), Dublin 2,* ☎ *676 3071.* Occasional performances of international drama.

Gaiety, *South King St, Dublin 2,* ☎ *677 1717.* 19th c theatre splendidly restored to its red plush and rococo charm. Two bars, one on ground floor, the other on first floor, are worth seeing for decor. Year-round performances of drama and variety, often with star names.

Gate, *Cavendish Row, Parnell Sq, Dublin 1,* ☎ *874 4045.* Arguably Dublin's most exciting theatre. Its reputation, from the peak of the ancient MacLiammor/Edwards regime, has been more than fully restored.

Olympia, *Dame St, Dublin 2,* ☎ *677 7444.* Once an old-time music hall, this is Dublin's oldest theatre (its origins date back even further than the Gaiety). It has been lovingly restored to its late 19th c splendour. Year-round selection of drama, revue and variety.

Peacock, *Lower Abbey St, Dublin 1,* ☎ *878 7222.* Basement theatre in Abbey theatre building. Irish language and experimental work. Café.

Players' Theatre, *No 3 Trinity College, Dublin 2,* ☎ *677 4673.* Excellent performances of student drama.

Point Theatre, *Point Depot, North Wall Quay, Dublin 1,* ☎ *836 3633.* Venue for celebrity entertainment events.

Project Arts Centre, *39 East Essex St, Dublin 2,* ☎ *671 2321.* Avant garde productions, usually very lively.

Riverbank Theatre, *Merchant's Quay, Dublin 8,* ☎ *677 3370.* Occasional performances. 10 mins walk from O'Connell Bridge.

Tivoli Theatre, *Francis St, Dublin 8,* ☎ *453 5998.* Interesting new venue.

FESTIVALS

During the summer months, Dublin has a plethora of festivals and events, mainly of a sporting nature. Throughout the rest of the year, there are many minor festivals, mainly devoted to music. Local TIOs have full details. St Patrick's Day on 17 March is designed for a local audience, but with the US very much in mind. One of the most interesting local festivals in the Dublin area is that for Dun Laoghaire, usually held in June, which features a good blend of cultural and sporting events. 16 June is Bloomsday and is now the most celebrated literary festival of the Dublin year, even though it is only for one day. In the autumn, the major festival is for Dublin Theatre, where every possible venue is pressed into service and an enormous variety of theatrical performances is offered.

1 Jan: Bank holiday. Jan – Mar, rugby internationals, Lansdowne Rd.

17 Mar: Bank holiday, St Patrick's Day. Parades, other events.

Mar/Apr: Good Friday, Easter Monday bank holidays. Variable dates.

April: Spring season of Opera. Irish Grand National.

1 May: Bank holiday.

16 June: Bloomsday (James Joyce) celebrations.

June: Dublin International Organ festival. Co Wicklow Gardens Festival. Budweiser Irish Derby, The Curragh. Festival of Music in Great Irish Houses.

July: Liffey powerboat racing, Dublin regatta. Dun Laoghaire Festival.

1 Aug: Bank holiday.

Aug: Antique Dealers' Fair. Horse Show, RDS.

Sept: All Ireland Football and Hurling finals (GAA).

Sept/Oct: Dublin Theatre festival.

31 Oct: Bank holiday.

Oct/Nov: Dublin Film festival.

Nov: Dublin International Indoor Horse Show, RDS.

Dec: Winter Opera season. Funderland, RDS (until Jan).

25 Dec: Public holiday, Christmas Day.

26 Dec: Bank holiday, St Stephen's Day. Wren Boys, revival of ancient Christmas custom.

FREE DUBLIN

Dublin is a moderately expensive city by world standards. However, there is a reasonable selection of things to do in and around the city that cost absolutely nothing. In the case of visits to the

Guinness and Irish whiskey museums, free refreshments are provided.

Bank of Ireland, *College Green, Dublin 2.* Once the seat of the Irish Houses of Parliament. Visitors will be shown round free of charge. *Mon−Fri, 10 a.m.−3 p.m. (Thurs, until 5 p.m.).*

Dunsink Observatory, *Castleknock, Co Dublin.* One of the oldest in the world, has occasional open nights. *Sept−Mar, 1st and 3rd Sats, 8 p.m.−10 p.m. For tickets, write to the Secretary. ☎ 838 7911. 40C bus from city centre to end of Dunsink Lane, Finglas South, then 0.8 km (0.5 mile) walk.*

Forbairt, *Ballymun Rd, Dublin 9.* Occasional open days of scientific interest. *☎ 837 0101. 11, 11A, 11B, 13, 19A buses from city centre.*

Four Courts, *Inns Quay, Dublin 7.* Visitors may attend court sittings in the Supreme and High Courts. *Mon−Fri. 15 mins walk from O'Connell Bridge. 25, 26 buses from city centre.*

Geological Survey of Ireland, *Beggar's Bush, Haddington Rd, Dublin 4.* Occasional exhibitions on geology and related subjects. *☎ 660 9511. 5, 7, 8, 45 buses from city centre to Northumberland Rd.*

Guinness Hop Store, *Crane St, off Thomas St, Dublin 8.* The ground-floor bar serves the firm's renowned dark beer free of charge to visitors. *☎ 453 3645. Mon−Sat, 10 a.m.−5.30 p.m., Sun, 2.30 p.m.−5.30 p.m. 21A, 78A, 123 buses from Fleet St to Thomas St.*

The Irish Times, *11-13 D'Olier St, Dublin 2.* Ultra-modern, high technology newspaper offices. Most interesting time is around midnight, when the huge full-colour press starts to roll for the following morning's editions. *Group tours by arr. ☎ 679 2022.*

Irish Whiskey Corner, *Bow St, Dublin 7.* Free whiskey in the Ball o' Malt bar, in conjuction with daily tours. *Mon−Fri, 3.30 p.m. Otherwise by arr. ☎ 872 5566. 34 bus from city centre to Church St.*

Marlay Craft Courtyard, *Rathfarnham.* Drop into this cluster of craft workshops to see fascinating crafts vigorously revived. Crafts represented include bookbinding, clockmaking, copper work, glassware, jewellery, musical instruments, pottery, sign-making and tapestry. *Workshops, Mon−Fri, shop* ☎ *494 2083. Mon−Sun. 47B bus from city centre.*

National Gallery of Ireland, *Merrion Sq, Dublin 2.* Conducted tours, also lectures, usually Suns, occasionally mid-week. ☎ *661 5133.*

Rathborne's Candle Factory, *East Wall Rd, Dublin 3.* Oldest company in Ireland, established in 1488. *Occasional visits by arr.* ☎ *874 3515/874 9222. 53 bus from city centre.*

RTE, *Donnybrook, Dublin 4.* RTE occasionally invites audiences for some TV shows. ☎ *208 3111.*

Teagasc, *19 Sandymount Ave, Dublin 4.* Organisation specialising in food research has occasional open days at its scientific stations in the Dublin area. ☎ *668 8188.*

Tower Design Centre, IDA *Enterprise Centre, Pearse St, Dublin 2.* Initially built as a sugar refinery, in 1862, the tower is now Ireland's largest craft and design centre. Over 30 workshops produce handknitting, stained glass, weaving, wood carving and many other artefacts. Shop and display area, café. ☎ *677 5655.*

GENEALOGY

Finding your Irish ancestors can provide much interest for the dedicated. A whole cottage industry has grown up in Dublin devoted to this service. Good starting points are the National Library, *Kildare St, Dublin 2* (it's so popular that you are advised to be there for the 10 a.m. opening in summer) and the new Genealogical Office close by. Other sources of documents are listed below. A number of professional genealogical research companies operate in Dublin. For details, contact the Association of Professional Genealogists, *24 Balnagowan, Palmerstown Park, Dublin 6,* ☎ *496 6522.* Several specialised bookshops, such as the Genealogy Bookshop, *3 Nassau St, Dublin 2,* ☎ *679 5313,* have useful advice and material.

Genealogical Office, *2 Kildare St, Dublin 2.* Reference material on genealogy; official pedigrees, coats of arms, will abstracts of wealthy families. ☎ *661 8811. Mon−Fri, 10 a.m.−12.30 p.m., 2 p.m.−4.30 p.m.*

National Library, *Kildare St, Dublin 2.* Much genealogical material, also extensive pre-1880 Catholic records of baptisms, births and marriages. ☎ *661 8811.*

Public Record Office, *Four Courts, Dublin 1.* Many useful records including survey of land ownership and leases, 1850s. ☎ *873 3833. Mon−Fri, 10 a.m.−5 p.m. Documents not produced between 12.45 p.m. and 2 p.m.*

Registrar General, *Joyce House, 8-11 Lombard St E, Dublin 2.* Register of births, marriages and deaths from 1864; non-Catholic marriages from 1845. ☎ *671 1968/671 1974. Mon−Fri, 9.30 a.m.− 12.30 p.m.; 2.15 p.m.−4.30 p.m.*

Registry of Deeds, *Henrietta St, Dublin 1.* Property records date from 1708. ☎ *874 8911. Mon−Fri, 10 a.m.−4.30 p.m.*

Valuation Office, *6 Ely Place, Dublin 2.* Valuable records of land ownership and leases from 1850s. ☎ *676 3211.*

NORTHERN IRELAND

If your ancestors came from the six counties that now comprise Northern Ireland, the **Public Records Office,** *66 Balmoral Ave, Belfast BT9 6NY* will help, ☎ *661621.* Also **Presbyterian Historical Society** at *Church House, Fisherwick Place, Belfast 1,* ☎ *323936,* and **Registrar General's Office,** *Oxford House, 49 Chichester St, Belfast BT1 4HL,* ☎ *235211.*

HISTORIC PLACES

These are mostly buildings of antiquity and interest; also listed are locations such as cemeteries, which are themselves redolent of Ireland's ancient and vexed history.

Alliance Française, *corner Kildare St and South Leinster St.* Once housed the magnificent Kildare Street Club. A few traces remain of the original architectural style.

Arbour Hill Cemetery, *Arbour Hill, Dublin 7.* Executed 1916

Easter Rising leaders are buried here. Other Irishmen who died in the Rising are also commemorated. *37, 39 buses to Stoneybatter.*

Bank of Ireland, *College Green (opp Trinity College), Dublin 2.* Construction started in 1729 on what was the first great 18th c edifice of Dublin. Until the Act of Union, which joined Ireland and Britain as a political entity, was passed in 1800, the Irish Houses of Parliament were located here. See the very finely decorated House of Lords, also old banknotes. *Mon – Fri, 10 a.m. – 4 p.m. Thurs, until 5 p.m.*

Bewley's City Centre Cafés. Redolent with Dublin atmosphere. South Great George's St is the oldest (late 19th c), while the Westmoreland St café dates back to 1916. Grafton St café was opened, extravagantly, in 1927. The magnificent Harry Clarke stained-glass windows (influenced by those in Chartres Cathedral) will encourage you to linger over your coffee. This café has interesting company museum.

Broadstone, *Dublin 7.* Old railway station with impressive façade. Built in 1850 as terminus for Midland & Great Western railway, closed in 1937. Now used as bus depot.

Casino, *Malahide Rd, Dublin 3.* Exquisite 18th c architectural gem. In recent years, it has been restored to its original magnificence, complete with furniture and furnishings. Good views from the roof. *June – Sept, daily, 9.30 a.m. – 6 p.m.* ☎ *833 1618. 9, 20A, 20B, 24, 27, 27A, 27B, 32A, 42, 42B buses from city centre.*

Castletown House, *Celbridge.* Magnificently restored 18th c mansion approached by 800-metres long lime tree avenue. In the house, see Long Gallery, with Venetian chandeliers, main hall and staircase. Also print room and Red Drawing Room. Some splendid Italian plasterwork, ☎ *628 8252. Apr – Sept, Mon – Fri, 10 a.m. – 6 p.m., Sun, BH, 2 p.m. – 6 p.m. 67, 67A, 67X buses from Middle Abbey St, Dublin, every hour. Journey time: 1¼ hrs.*

Celbridge Abbey, *16 km (10 miles) W of Dublin.* Now a home for mentally handicapped children, it was once home of Esther van Homrigh, Jonathan Swift's 'Vanessa'. The grounds, beside the River Liffey, have been developed into a substantial amenity,

including theme walks, riverside walks, model railway, tra┌
in a donkey-drawn carriage, garden centre and tea ro┌
Mar−Oct, Tues−Sun and bank holidays, 12 noon−6 p.m. ☎
628 8350. 67, 67A buses. Frequent train service from Connolly Station, Dublin.

City Hall, *Dame St, Dublin 2.* Built between 1769 and 1779, it is now the headquarters of Dublin Corporation. Contains 102 Royal Charters and the mace and sword of city. Impressive circular entrance hall. *Mon−Fri, 9.30 a.m.−5 p.m. Walk from Trinity College.*

Clontarf Castle, *Clontarf, Dublin 3.* Main building was constructed in 1835 with mahogany staircase, carvings and panellings. Tower of original 12th c castle still intact. Main building now used as restaurant/entertainment centre, ☎ *833 2271/833 1898. 29A, 30, 31A, 44A buses from city centre to Castle Ave.*

Cook Street, *(between Thomas St and quays), Dublin 8.* Imposing, but greatly restored section of city walls; original sections dated back around eight centuries. *21A, 78A, 123 buses from city centre to Thomas St.*

Custom House, *Custom House Quay.* Not open to visitors, but the finely restored late 18th c façade may be admired while strolling along the riverside.

Donnybrook Burial Ground, *Donnybrook Rd,. Dublin 4.* Small graveyard, on monastic site, next to garda barracks, contains remains of 18th c and 19th c Dublin notables. Heavily wooded, very atmospheric. *10, 46A buses to Donnybrook Rd.*

Drimnagh Castle, *Drimnagh, Dublin 12.* 13th c castle with moat still full of water. Following restoration, Great Hall, undercroft, gardens, yard and surrounding buildings are open. *Apr−Oct, Wed, Sat, Sun, 12 noon−5 p.m.* ☎ *450 2530. 18, 56A, 210 buses to CBS school, Long Mile Rd.*

Dublin Castle, *Dame St, Dublin 2.* Once the seat of British administration in Ireland. See the State apartments, including the vast St Patrick's Hall, with its lofty panelled ceiling. It's now used for State ocasions. Church of the Most Holy Trinity has magnificent interior decorations; currently being renovated. Medieval under tage centre, shop and restaurant. *Mon−Fri,* *p.m. 2 p.m.−5 p.m. Sun, BH, 2 p.m.−5 p.m.*

ocational Educational Committee Offices, *corner of Anglesea/Merrion Rd, Ballsbridge, Dublin 4.* Once town hall of the old Pembroke township, included in Dublin in 1930. Plaque on front door recalls the connection. Adjacent archways once part of old Pembroke fire station in days of horse-drawn fire engines. *5, 7, 8, 45 buses to* RDS, DART *to Lansdowne Rd, 600 metres.*

Dublin Clubs. The last two traditional clubs, the Stephen's Green and the Hibernian United Services Club, next door to one another on St Stephen's Green (Grafton St end) have exquisite interior decorations. Worth asking to view.

Dublinia. Synod Hall beside Christchurch cathedral shows everyday life in medieval Dublin, using high tech means. Scale model of Dublin in 1500, medieval maze. *Apr−Sept, daily, 10 a.m.−5 p.m., Oct−Mar, Mon−Sat, 11 a.m.−4 p.m., Sun, 10 a.m.−4 p.m.* ☎ 679 4611.

Four Courts, *Inns Quay, Dublin 7.* Magnificent 18th c building, complete with majestic dome, completed by Gandon, the great architect of Georgian Dublin. Destroyed in 1922 during the civil war; included in the destruction were many public records. Later restored. Building now houses Supreme and High Courts. Visitors can see the entrance hall, beneath the dome. *Mon−Fri. 15 mins walk from O'Connell Bridge.*

General Post Office, *O'Connell St, Dublin 1.* 1916 Easter Rising started here. Present building is a post-1916 reconstruction of early 19th c edifice. Statue of the Dying Cuchulainn, a figure from Celtic mythology, is in main concourse.

Glasnevin Cemetery, *Dublin 11.* The city's answer to Père Lachaise in Paris. Many of Ireland's most famous dead are buried here, including political figures from O'Donovan Rossa, James Devoy and Jim Larkin to Sir Roger Casement, Eamon de Valera and Sean MacBride. *40, 40A, 40B, 40C buses from city centre.*

Grangegorman Military Cemetery, *Blackhorse Ave, Dublin 7.* British forces were buried here from late 19th c, including soldiers killed in 1916 Easter Rising and 600 other servicemen from World War I. *10, 37 buses from city centre to Blackhorse Ave.*

Harcourt Street Station, *Harcourt St, Dublin 2.* The railway line to Bray was opened in 1859 and closed in 1959. The station's distinguished architecture may be seen from the outside. Parts of the old railway line may be followed through Ranelagh, Dundrum and Foxrock.

Huguenot Cemetery, *Merrion Row, Dublin 2.* Many French Huguenots who settled in Dublin in the 18th c are buried in this restored cemetery.

James Joyce Cultural Centre, *35 North Great George's St, off Parnell St, Dublin 1.* Authentic restoration of 18th c house as Joycean centre, complete with library, exhibitions, lectures. ☎ *873 1984.*

James Joyce Tower, *Sandycove, Co Dublin.* Good collection of Joyce material. Occasional lectures. Excellent views from roof. *May 30 – Sept 1, Mon – Sat, 10 a.m. – 5 p.m., Sun, 2 p.m. – 6 p.m. Otherwise by arr., ☎ 280 9625/280 8571. 8 bus from Dublin, every 20 mins. Journey time: 45 mins.* DART *to Sandycove station.*

King's Inns, *Henrietta St, Dublin 7.* Magnificent classical building designed at close of 18th c. Dining hall and library are very fine; latter has over 100,000 volumes and nearly 10,000 pamphlets. Normally, only members of the legal profession are permitted entry. Gardens open to public, ☎ *874 4840. 19, 19A, 34 buses from city centre to Broadstone.*

Leinster House, *Kildare St, Dublin 2.* Sandwiched between the National Library and the National Museum, this building was constructed in 1745 for the Duke of Leinster. At the time, the south city was very unfashionable, while Capel St and Mountjoy Sq were the popular areas. In 1815, the Royal Dublin Society (now housed in Ballsbridge) took over the building. Since 1922, it has housed the two chambers of the Irish parliament. Ticket applications should be made to a member of the Dáil or Seanad, through the visitor's embassy, or to the Superintendent's Office in Kildare St. *Mon – Fri.*

29 Lower Fitzwilliam Street: another excellent restoration by the Electricity Supply Board, this time of an 18th c house complete with all domestic fittings. *Tues – Sat, 10 a.m. – 5 p.m., Sun, 2 p.m. – 5 p.m.* ☎ *706 6165.*

Malahide Castle, *Malahide, Dublin 5.* Many features worth seeing, including Great Hall, Front Hall, Oak Room, Library and Drawing Room. Fine furniture, panelling and National Portrait Collection. Concerts, craft, antique shop, guided tours. Extensive parkland with sporting facilities, picnic areas, nature trails, Botanic Gardens. The Fry model railway museum has a unique collection of models of Irish trains. *All year, Mon – Fri, 10 a.m. – 5 p.m., Sat, Sun, BH, 2 p.m. – 5 p.m.* ☎ *845 2337. 32A, 42, 102, 230 buses from Dublin every 45 mins. Journey time: 45 mins. Frequent trains from Connolly station, Dublin.*

Mansion House, *Dawson St, Dublin 2.* Queen Anne-style house dates from 1710. Now official home of Lord Mayor of Dublin. Interesting internal architecture. *By arr.* ☎ *676 1845.*

Masonic Hall, *Molesworth St, Dublin 2.* 19th c building has interesting internal design and statuary. *By arr.* ☎ *676 1337.*

Memorial Park, *Islandbridge, Dublin 8.* Elaborate Lutyens designed memorial, now renovated, commemorates fallen British servicemen, especially from World War I, when 50,000 Irish recruits died in British army. Pleasant riverside location. *Open daylight hours. 68, 69, 70 buses from city centre to Inchicore Rd.*

Mountjoy Square, *Dublin 1.* Dublin's first Georgian square. In mid-18th c, it was the city's most fashionable area, but later, as fashion swung south of the River Liffey, Mountjoy Sq went into near-terminal decline. Only the buildings on two sides remain in good condition; otherwise, much dereliction.

Newman House, *85 – 86 St Stephen's Green.* Splendid restoration of two 18th c Georgian houses, where University College, Dublin, began in 19th c. Range of rooms includes suitably formal Bishops' Room. Video history. *June – Sept, Tues – Fri, 10 a.m. – 4.30 p.m., Sat, 2 p.m. – 4.30 p.m., Sun, 11 a.m. – 2 p.m.* ☎ *475 7255/475 1752.* Iveagh Gardens to rear.

Parliament Street, *Dublin 2.* One of the city's oldest thorough-fares, now rather decrepit. At top right-hand corner, opp. City Hall, see old Dublin *Evening Mail* building, one of Dublin's great newspapers, which closed down in 1962. Also in Parliament St, Dublin's oldest shop, Read's cutlers, dating back to 1670.

Pearse Station, *Westland Row, Dublin 2.* Ireland's first railway station, which was built in 1834. The first railway line ran as far as the West Pier in Kingstown (now Dun Laoghaire).

Rathfarnham Castle, *Dublin 16.* Castle dates back to at least late 16th c, extensive restoration nearly completed. Building is open to visitors and now has café. *All year, daily, 10 a.m. − 6 p.m. 16, 16A, 17, 47 buses.*

Royal Hospital, *Kilmainham, Dublin 8.* Built over three centuries ago to house military pensioners, it was based on Les Invalides, Paris. Closed in 1927, it lay derelict for many years until a £20 million restoration programme began in 1978. Great Hall chapel is particularly worth seeing. Now used as a national centre for culture and the arts, with many concerts, exhibitions, lectures and tours. Also open-air theatre. Adjoining Irish Museum of Modern Art. Brunch is served in the cellar, *Sun,* ☎ *671 8666. Daily, all year. 26, 51, 79, 90 buses from Aston Quay to Heuston station.*

Russborough House, *Blessington, Co Wicklow.* One of Ireland's finest houses, built in classical style between 1740 and 1750. Magnificent paintings, plasterwork, bronzes, carpets, furniture and porcelain. Woodland gardens, ☎ *(045) 65239. Easter − Oct, Sun, BH, 2.30 p.m. − 5.30 p.m. June − Aug, Mon − Sat, 10.30 a.m. − 5.30 p.m. 65 bus from Crampton Quay, Dublin, every 1½ hrs. Journey time: 1½ hrs.*

Shaw House, *33 Synge St, Dublin 8 (off South Cicular Rd).* George Bernard Shaw's birthplace has been authentically restored. *May − Sept, Mon − Sat, 10 a.m. − 5 p.m., Sun, BH, 2 p.m. − 6 p.m.* ☎ *872 1490. 19, 19A, 22, 22A, 54 buses to Harrington St.*

St Mary's Abbey, *Meetinghouse Lane, off Capel St, Dublin 1.* Only the ruins of the Chapter House remain of this once great 12th c abbey, the oldest foundation in the city. Silken Thomas started his insurrection here against the English in 1534. *June – Sept, Wed, 10 a.m. – 5 p.m.* ☎ *872 1490*.

Straffan, *Co Kildare*. Steam museum has fascinating, working models and old steam engines. Shop, tea-room. *Feb – Oct,* ☎ *627 3155*. Butterfly farm: *1 May – Aug, BH, daily, 12 noon – 5.30 p.m.* ☎ *627 1109*.

Tailors' Hall, *Back Lane, Dublin 8*. Set in the Liberties, this building, nearly 300-years old, is Dublin's only surviving guild-hall. Extensively restored, with magnificent great hall featuring list of all masters of the tailor's guild from its first charter in 1419 to its abolition in 1841. Now headquarters of An Taisce, the National Trust for Ireland, ☎ *454 1786. 21A, 78A, 123 buses to Cornmarket*.

Trinity College, *Dublin 2*. Founded in 1592 by Queen Elizabeth I, many of the present-day college buildings date from the 18th c and 19th c. The Front Square, laid out with cobblestones, the Bell Tower, and the old and new libraries are just some of the architectural highlights. College grounds open Mon – Sun. 'The Dublin Experience', a multi-media presentation on the history of Dublin and Trinity College, takes place in the Arts and Social Science building *(All week, summer only)*. The Colonnades is a new exhibition area below the old library.

Wood Quay, *Dublin 8*. Now occupied by modern buildings of Dublin Corporation, this was the site of the original Viking town. Site excavation revealed extensive remains from 9th c to 11th c. Despite widespread protests, construction work on the new buildings went ahead.

LIBRARIES

Dublin is richly endowed with libraries. Some are municipally owned, while others are private. The most interesting libraries, from an architectural and bibliographic point of view, are Marsh's library, the National Library of Ireland, the Royal Irish Academy library and Trinity College (where the Book of Kells is stored). Dublin's newest library is the space age institution in the ILAC centre.

Anglesea Road Branch Library, *Ballsbridge, Dublin 4.* Attractive library with much material on Dublin, occasional exhibitions. Death mask of Frank O'Connor, short story writer, on view, ☎ *668 9575. 5, 7, 8, 45 buses to* RDS. DART *to Lansdowne Rd, 600 metres.*

Book of Kells, *Trinity College.* One of the world's most famous books is to be found in the Colonnades exhibition area, old library, together with other medieval masterpieces. Well-stocked shop. *All year, Mon—Fri, 9.30 a.m.—4.45 p.m., Sat, 9.30 a.m.— 12.45 p.m.* ☎ *677 2941.*

Central Catholic Library, *74 Merrion Sq, Dublin 2.* 80,000 volumes of general and religious interest, large Irish section. Lending and reference departments, reading room. ☎ *676 1264. Lending section, Mon—Sat, 12 noon—7 p.m. Reference section, Mon—Sat, 11 a.m.—7.30 p.m.*

Chester Beatty Library and Gallery of Oriental Art, *20 Shrewsbury Rd, Dublin 4.* Outstanding collection of books, paintings, papyri, clay tablets, bindings, wall hangings, costumes, carvings and drawings, illustrating history of mankind from 2700 BC (Babylonian clay tablets) to present day. Vast array of Japanese prints, plus one of world's outstanding collections of Islamic art. Due to relocate to Dublin Castle. ☎ *269 2386. Tues—Fri, 10 a.m.—5 p.m. Sat, 2 p.m.—5 p.m. Guided tours, Wed, 2.30 p.m. 5, 7, 8, 45 buses from city centre to Shrewsbury Rd.* DART *to Sydney Parade, 700 metres.*

Dublin Diocesan Library, *Clonliffe Rd, Dublin 3.* Extensive reference facilities. ☎ *874 1680. Mon—Fri, 10.30 a.m.—9.30 p.m. Sat, 10.30 a.m.—1 p.m. 3, 11, 16, 36 buses from city centre.*

Goethe Institute, *37 Merrion Sq, Dublin 2.* Many books and other archive material of German interest. ☎ *661 1155. Mon, Tues, Thurs, 4 p.m.—8 p.m. Wed, Fri, 10 a.m.—6 p.m. Sat, 10 a.m.— 1 p.m.*

ILAC Centre Library, *Henry St, Dublin 1.* Exciting range of services in ultra-modern library in shopping centre. Includes children's library, micro-computer use, video viewing and business information services. Regular concerts and lectures.

Tues – Thurs, 10 a.m. – 8 p.m. Fri, Sat, 10 a.m. – 5 p.m. ☎
873 4333.

Marsh's Library, *St Patrick's Close (behind St Patrick's Cathedral), Patrick St, Dublin 2.* Marvellous 1701 library with some 25,000 books. Certain books date back to 16th c and are so rare that readers used to be locked into cages to peruse them. Great atmosphere has been preserved in major restoration programme. Librarian, Mrs Muriel McCarthy, is a mine of information. ☎ *454 3511. Open all year. 10 mins walk from St Stephens Green, via Kevin St.*

National Library, *Kildare St, Dublin 2.* Recently renovated, it contains vast collection of Irish newspapers and magazines; virtually every issue of every title ever published is represented. More recent newspapers are on microfilm. Enormous collection of books published in Ireland. Very useful place for ancestor tracing. Frequent exhibitions. ☎ *661 8811. Mon, 10 a.m. – 9 p.m. Tues, Wed, 2 p.m. – 9 p.m. Thurs, Fri, 10 a.m. – 5 p.m. Sat, 10 a.m. – 1 p.m.*

Pearse St, *Dublin 2.* Gilbert collection has abundant material on Dublin history, including printing and bookbinding. ☎ *677 7662.*

Poetry Ireland, *Bermingham Tower, Upper Yard, Dublin Castle, Dublin 2.* Resource centre for poets and writers. Austin Clarke library has some 6,000 volumes collected by the poet in his lifetime; emphasis on Irish poetry, but also drama and fiction. Many out-of-print volumes. Book club, poetry readings. ☎ *671 4632. Mon – Fri, 2 p.m. – 5 p.m.*

Quaker Library, *Swanbrook House, off Morehampton Rd, Dublin 4.* Small library with wealth of historical material, printed and photographic, about the Quakers. *Thurs, 11 a.m. – 1 p.m.* ☎ *668 3686.*

Royal Dublin Society Library, *Ballsbridge, Dublin 4.* A fine collection of historic and scientific volumes. ☎ *668 0645. Mon – Fri, by arr. 5, 7, 8, 45 buses from city centre to* RDS. DART *to Lansdowne Rd, 600 metres.*

Royal Irish Academy Library, *Dawson St, Dublin 2.* One of largest collections of ancient Irish manuscripts in the country. *All year, Mon – Fri, 9.30 a.m. – 5.30 p.m. Closed lunchtime and most of Aug.* ☎ *676 4222.*

MUSEUMS

Dublin's two major museums are the National Museum of Ireland, which holds works of national importance, and the Civic Museum, which is more homely and directly related to the history of the city. In addition, many newer, smaller, museums have been added in recent years, some confined to specific areas of interest.

Army Archives, *Cathal Brugha Barracks, Lower Rathmines Rd, Dublin 6: records, memorabilia. By arr.* ☎ *497 5782. 14, 14A, 15A, 15B buses from city centre to barracks.*

Bray Museum, *Old Courthouse, Main St, Bray.* Many artefacts and mementoes of previous generations, including domestic utensils. Photographs of old Bray. *Open daily.* ☎ *286 7128. 45, 84 buses from city centre,* DART.

Civic Museum, *South William St, Dublin 2 (behind Grafton St).* Fascinating collection of items from the city's social history. Stone Age flint axes, Viking coins, old maps and prints, even Nelson's head from Nelson's Pillar, blown up in 1966. Frequent theme exhibitions. Also City Archives. *Tues – Sat, 10 a.m. – 6 p.m. Sun, 11 a.m. – 2 p.m.*
☎ *679 4260.*

Classical Museum, *University College, Belfield, Dublin 4.* Archaeological items from ancient Greece and Rome. *Fri, 1.30 p.m. – 2.30 p.m. By arr, Victor Connerty, curator,* ☎ *269 3244 ext 8218. 10 bus from city centre.*

Dublin Writers' Museum, *18-19 Parnell Square, Dublin 1.* Many mementoes of well-known Dublin writers. Exhibitions, bookshop, restaurant. *All year, Mon – Sat, 10 a.m. – 5 p.m. Sun, BH, 2 p.m. – 6 p.m.* ☎ *872 2077.*

Education Museum, *Church of Ireland College of Further Education, 94 Upper Rathmines Rd, Dublin 6.* The story of Ireland's schools, told through interactive displays. Includes a

19th c classroom. *Open all year, Wed, 2.30 p.m. −5.30 p.m.* ☎ *497 0033. 14, 14A buses.*

Findlaters, *10 Upper Hatch St, Dublin 2.* Wine vaults museum has many relics of wine trade and old Dublin history, including shops. *Mon−Sat, 9 a.m. −6 p.m.* ☎ *475 1699.*

Fry Model Railway, *Malahide Castle, Co Dublin.* Special museum houses one of world's major model railway layouts. Track totals 4.5 km (2.8 miles); features many models of old Dublin trains, buses, trams, even a Guinness barge. Restaurant in adjoining castle. *Open all year Mon−Fri, 10 a.m. −5 p.m. Sat, 11 a.m. −6 p.m. Sun, BH, 2 p.m. −6 p.m.* ☎ *845 2758. 42 bus from Dublin city centre. Train from Connolly station to Malahide.*

Garda Museum, *Garda headquarters, Phoenix Park, Dublin 8.* Illustrates history of gardai (Irish police) since they were established, with the Irish Free State, in 1922. Citations, medals, photographs, uniforms and other historical material. *By arr,* ☎ *677 1156. 10 bus from city centre to Phoenix Park.*

Guinness Museum, *Hop Store, Crane St, off Thomas St, Dublin 8.* Many exhibits detailing history of the firm both in Ireland and elsewhere in the world. *All year, Mon−Sat, 10 a.m. −5.30 p.m. Sun, 2.30 a.m. −5.30 p.m.* ☎ *453 6700. 21A, 78A, 123 buses from Fleet St.*

Heraldic Museum, *2 Kildare St, Dublin 2.* Founded in 1911. For many years it was located in Dublin Castle; now in larger premises, Kildare St. *Mon−Fri, 10 a.m. −12.30 p.m., 2 p.m. − 4.30 p.m.* ☎ *661 4877.*

Irish Architectural Archive, *73 Merrion Sq, Dublin 2.* 1793 Georgian house with much of its original decor well preserved, has much material, from drawings to models and photographs, portraying Irish architecture from late 16th c to present day, ☎ *676 3430. Mon−Fri, 10 a.m. −1 p.m.; 2 p.m. −5 p.m.*

Irish Horse Museum, *Kildare.* Many fascinating relics, including the skeleton of Arkle, the renowned Irish racehorse. The adjacent National Stud can also be visited. *All year, Mon−Fri, 10 a.m. − 5 p.m. Sat, 10 a.m. −6 p.m. Sun, 2 p.m. −6 p.m.* ☎ *(045) 21617.*

Irish Jewish Museum, *3-4 Walworth Rd, off Victoria St, Dublin 8.* Memorabilia of Ireland's Jewish community over the last 150 years. Restored synagogue. *May−Sept, Tues, Thurs, Sun, 11 a.m.−3.30 p.m. Oct−Apr, Sun, 10.30 a.m.−2.30 p.m.* ☎ *453 1797. 16, 19, 19A, 22, 55 buses from city centre to Harrington St.*

Irish Museum of Modern Art, *Royal Hospital, Kilmainham, Dublin 8.* Impressive collection of Irish and international art. Frequent exhibitions. *Tues−Sat, 10 a.m.−5.30 p.m. Sun, BH, 12 noon−5.30 p.m.* ☎ *671 8666.*

Irish Print Museum. Transferring to extensive new premises in the former Garrison Chapel at Beggar's Bush Barracks, Haddington Rd, Dublin 4. *Details:* ☎ *874 3662.*

Irish Railway Records Society, *Heuston Station, Dublin 8.* Relive bygone days of the Irish railways, when steam reigned supreme. Fine collection of photographs, press cuttings, etc. *Every Tues, 8 p.m. 26, 51, 79, 90 buses from city centre.*

Irish Whiskey Corner, *Irish Distillers, Bow St, Dublin 7.* Fascinating collection of whiskey memorabilia, including model distillery, copper pot still, model of old-time cooper, distillery implements, old bottles and labels, even list of coopers' nicknames. Adjacent Ball o' Malt bar is lined with old advertising mirrors. *Usually daily tour, Mon−Fri, 3.30 p.m., but check first,* ☎ *872 5566. 34 bus from city centre to Church St.*

Joyce Museum, *Sandycove, Co Dublin.* The Martello Tower contains a museum with material on one of the world's leading 20th c writers.

Kilmainham Jail, *Inchicore, Dublin 8.* Old prison, where leaders of 1916 Easter Rising were held and later executed, has been restored and turned into a museum of the War of Independence period. The cells where Pearse and others were held and yard where they were executed are particularly eerie. Also audio-visual presentation. *May−Sept, daily, 10 a.m.−6 p.m. Oct−Apr, Mon−Fri, Sun, 1 p.m.−6 p.m.* ☎ *453 5984. 79 bus from city centre to Inchicore Rd.*

Ledwidge Museum, *Slane, Co Meath.* Francis Ledwidge, local poet who was killed in World War I and whose work is increasingly appreciated, was born in this cottage, now turned into museum full of nostalgic mementoes. ☎ *(041) 25201. Mar − Oct, Mon, Tues, Wed, 10 a.m. − 6 p.m. Otherwise by arr. Bus 3 times daily from Dublin; journey time: 45 mins. Bus 4 times daily from Drogheda; journey time: 20 mins.*

Lusk Heritage Centre, *Lusk, Co Dublin.* Local history museum in old church, adjacent round tower. *Mid June − Sept, daily, 10 a.m. − 6 p.m. Or by arr,* ☎ *843 7683.*

Millmount Museum, *Drogheda.* One of Ireland's best town museums, full of fascinating relics of old Drogheda, from craft instruments to old union banners. Adjacent tower, if gate open, gives magnificent views over whole town. *Summer, daily, 10 a.m. − 1 p.m., 2 p.m. − 5 p.m. Winter, Wed, Sat, Sun, 3 p.m. − 5 p.m.* ☎ *(041) 36391. Train from Connolly station, Dublin, every 2 hrs.*

Museum of Childhood, *20 Palmerston Park, Dublin 6.* Wonderful collection of dolls from early 18th c onwards. Also miniature furniture, rocking horses and prams. Regular exhibitions. *Jul − Aug, Wed, Sun, 2 p.m. − 5.30 p.m., Sept − June, Sun, 2 p.m. − 5.30 p.m., or by arr,* ☎ *497 3223. 14, 14A buses from city centre.*

National Archives, *Bishop St, Dublin 8:* government papers, 1922 − 60. *Mon − Fri, 10 a.m. − 5 p.m.,* ☎ *478 3711. 16, 16A, 19, 19A, 22, 22A, 53, 83 buses to Wexford St.*

National Maritime Museum, *Haigh Terrace, Dun Laoghaire.* Church converted into very interesting museum of the sea. Many models of ships, French longboat captured at Bantry in 1796. Working optic from Baily lighthouse, Howth. *May − Sept, Tues − Sun, 2.30 p.m. − 5.30 p.m. Oct − Apr, Sat, Sun, 2.30 p.m. − 5.30 p.m.* ☎ *280 0969. 7, 7A, 8 buses from Dublin to Dun Laoghaire.* DART *to Dun Laoghaire station.*

National Museum, *Kildare St, Dublin 2.* The treasury has an audio-visual presentation on ancient Irish art, up to the 15th c. Items include the Ardagh Chalice and the Cross of Cong. Viking Dublin display. Material on Easter Rising 1916 and War of Independence. Other sections include ceramics, coins, glass, porcelain and silver. The museum has a small Japanese collection and a music room, with instruments dating back to 1100. Much of the museum is being relocated to Collins Barracks near Heuston station. *All year, Tues — Sat, 10 a.m. — 5 p.m. Sun, 2 p.m. — 5 p.m.* Same opening times for new exhibition section, Merrion Row. ☎ *661 8811, 660 1117 (Merrion Row).*

National Wax Museum, *Granby Row, off Parnell Sq, Dublin 1.* Many Irish and international personalities, from the Pope to Ian Paisley, are modelled in wax. Some spooky side-shows, too. Includes Sam Mellowes GAA museum, with collection of autographed hurleys and football boots of famous players. *Mon — Sat, 10 a.m. — 5.30 p.m. (6 p.m. in summer), Sun, 12 noon — 6 p.m.* ☎ *872 6340.*

Natural History Museum, *Merrion Sq, Dublin 2.* Fine collection of animals and birds indigenous to Ireland. *Tues — Sat, 10 a.m. — 5 p.m., Sun, 2 p.m. — 5 p.m.* ☎ *661 8811.*

Pearse Museum, *St Enda's Park, Rathfarnham, Dublin 16.* Patrick Pearse, 1916 Easter Rising leader, was headmaster at St Enda's school set in this 18th c house. Interesting memorabilia. Large park with nature trail. *Nov — Jan, daily, 10 a.m. — 1 p.m.; 2 p.m. — 4 p.m. Feb — Apr, Sept, Oct, daily, 10 a.m. — 1 p.m.; 2 p.m. — 5 p.m. May — Aug, daily, 10 a.m. — 1 p.m.; 2 p.m. — 5.30 p.m.* ☎ *493 4208. 16 bus from city centre.*

St Patrick's College Museum, *Maynooth, Co Kildare.* Items include horse-shoeing machine and the battery invented by Rev Dr Nicholas Callan, 19th c professor of science here. Historical ecclesiastical items. *Summer, Tues, Thur, 2 p.m. — 4 p.m. Sun, 2 p.m. — 5 p.m.* ☎ *628 5222. 66, 67A buses from Dublin every 20 mins. Journey time: 50 mins. Train from Connolly station, Dublin. Journey time: 30 mins.*

St Patrick's Hospital, *off James's St (near Guinness brewery).* Built with 18th c legacy from Dean Swift. Treasure trove of Swiftiana, including the desk at which he is reputed to have written *Gulliver's Travels,* is located in a new display area. *By arr,* ☎ *677 5423. 21A, 78A, 123 buses from city centre to James's St.*

Swords Museum, *Swords, Co Dublin.* Located in Carnegie

library; many interesting items on history of north Co Dublin. *Sun, 2.30 p.m. − 6 p.m. 33, 41, 41B, 230 buses every 20 mins from Eden Quay, Dublin. Journey time: 50 mins.*

Transport Museum, *Howth Castle grounds, Howth.* Antique passenger vehicles, including Hill of Howth tram and 1937 Dublin double-deck bus, and commercial vehicles, including 1927 lorry used in film *Ryan's Daughter,* and a 1889 steam fire engine. ☎ *847 5623. All year, Sat, Sun, BH, 2 p.m. − 5 p.m. 31, 31B buses.* DART *from Connolly station.*

Trinity College, *Dublin 2.* Three departmental museums have material of interest, covering biblical antiquities, geology and zoology. The Closet Press has antique printing equipment and materials. Also, the 18th c Printing House has old equipment from the Cuala Press, founded early this century by W. B. Yeats's sister. *By arr with each individual collection.* ☎ *677 2941.*

Waterways Visitor Centre, *Grand Canal Quay, off Pearse St, Dublin 2.* History of Ireland's inland waterways is explained in ultra-modern high tech centre. *Open Jun − Sept, daily, 9.30 a.m. − 6.30 p.m.* ☎ *677 7510. 3 bus.*

NEAR DUBLIN

Bettystown, *48 km (30 miles) N of Dublin.* 10 km (6 miles) long golden strand. Horse racing on strand, July. Village Hotel has century-old photographs taken in vicinity. Summer fun fair in village. Nearby River Boyne estuary, also Mornington village with Moran's traditional pub. *Frequent train from Connolly station, Dublin to Drogheda. Journey time: 1 hr. Also bus every 2 hrs from Drogheda. Journey time: 30 mins.*

Blackrock, *8 km (5 miles) SE of Dublin.* Seashore park. 2 shopping centres, one with fine bookshop. Wide array of other shops, restaurants. House in nearby Carysfort Ave was one of 23 once occupied in Dublin area by James Joyce. Dublin Crystal Glass, *Carysfort Ave,* ☎ *288 7932. 5, 7, 7A, 8, 17, 45 buses.* DART.

Blessington, *29 km (18 miles) SW of Dublin.* Pleasant village with tree-lined Main St. Easy walk to shores of Poulaphouca Lake, with lakeside walks, boating, fishing. Hollywood Glen, 6 km (4 miles) S has attractive walks. Russborough House (*see* HISTORIC PLACES). Blessington Lakes leisure centre. *65 bus from Dublin every 1½ hrs. Journey time: 1½ hrs.*

Bray, *21 km (13 miles) S of Dublin.* Lengthy esplanade offers excellent walks. Crowded in summer, but in winter hit by dramatic storms when waves wash over the front. The seafront has also been punctuated by a recently built aquarium. Several amusement arcades line landward side. Harbour at N end of town; Harbour Bar has good atmosphere, old mirrors and photographs. Interesting lane-ways, streets and squares between front and Main St. Town Hall has been renovated; new heritage centre (*see* MUSEUMS). *Buses every 40 mins from city centre. Journey time: 1 hr.* DART *from Connolly/Pearse stations, every 15/20 mins. Journey time: 40 mins.*

Dalkey, *13 km (8 miles) SW of Dublin.* Seaside resort with two harbours, Bulloch and Coliemore. Town has been immortalised by Flann O'Brien and Hugh Leonard (the latter lives in Dalkey). Archibald's Castle, Castle St and tower, opp, are only remaining remnants of once extensive medieval fortifications. Torca Cottage (*see* BLUE PLAQUES). Dalkey Island trips (*see* UNUSUAL EXCURSIONS). Walk to Vico Rd (*see* WALKS). *8 bus from Dublin, also* DART *to Dalkey station.*

Delgany, *32 km (20 miles) S of Dublin.* Small village with exceptional walks along secluded roads. 18th c church (*see* CHURCHES). Three pubs (Delgany Inn, Horse & Hound, Wicklow Arms) provide inner sustenance after those enticing walks. *84 bus every hr from College St, Dublin. Journey time: 1½ hrs.*

Drogheda, *48 km (30 miles) N of Dublin.* Hilly town on banks of River Boyne. Dates back 2,000 years. Captured by Cromwell in 1649. Although recent roadworks have cut a swathe through the town, back lanes and quaysides remain of interest. St Peter's Church (C), West St, has shrine of St Oliver Plunkett, martyred London 1681. Jewelled casket containing his head is venerated during pilgrimages. St Mary's (CI), top of Peter St, fine views of town from graveyard. Augustinian Abbey, Abbey Lane: only the 13th c tower still stands. Sienna Convent, Chord Road, has air of great peace. Millmount Museum (*see* MUSEUMS). Courthouse, *Fair St*. Has sword and mace presented to Drogheda Corporation by William III after Battle of the Boyne. *By arr, Town Clerk's office, Mon – Fri. Express buses from Busarus, Dublin, every 2 hrs. Journey time: 1½ hrs. Frequent train from Connolly station, Dublin. Journey time: 30 mins – 1 hr.*

Duleek, *40 km (25 miles) N of Dublin.* Remains of ruined 13th c priory, also ancient bridge across River Nanny, with plaque dated 1587 in parapet. *Bus from Busarus, Dublin, twice daily. Bus every 3 hrs from Drogheda. Journey time: from Dublin 1 hr, from Drogheda 20 mins.*

Dun Laoghaire, *11 km (7 miles) SW of Dublin.* Seaside town and ferry port, first landing in Ireland for many people arriving by car ferry. Two piers offer excellent walks. Some terraces in the town have a certain neo-Georgian charm. National Maritime Museum, Haigh Terrace (*see* MUSEUMS). Dun Laoghaire shopping centre has many shops on several levels, also restaurants. Top-floor pub has good views across Dublin Bay. At Dun Laoghaire station, part of building converted into exquisite Restaurant na Mara. *7, 8, 46A buses from Dublin, also* DART.

Enniskerry, *19 km (12 miles) SW of Dublin.* Pretty village in wooded hollow, village square. Nearby Glen of the Dargle. Powerscourt gardens and waterfall (*see* PARKS AND GARDENS). *44 bus from Dublin every 1½ hrs. Journey time: 1½ hrs.*

Greystones, *29 km (18 miles) SW of Dublin.* Fine walk around small harbour and along seafront. Popular in summer, deserted in winter. La Touche Hotel has interesting century-old documents and photographs of the hotel's construction and the locality. Walk along Church Road to Church of Ireland church, set in wooded area. Beach starts at S end of town and runs for 13 km (8 miles); good shore fishing. *84 bus from College St, Dublin, every hr. Journey time: 1¼ hrs.* DART *to Bray, every 15/20 mins, then connecting feeder train or 84A bus to Greystones. Total journey time from Dublin: 1 hr.*

Hill of Tara, *45 km (28 miles) NW of Dublin.* Historic, scenic sight, interpretative centre in old Church of Ireland church. *Opening times,* TIO. *Bus from Busaras.*

Howth, *16 km (10 miles) N of Dublin.* Seaside village with marina. Popular summer resort. Ancient Abbey Tavern (*see* PUBS). Howth Castle gardens (*see* PARKS AND GARDENS). Transport museum (*see* MUSEUMS). Local art galleries have shows by local artists. *31, 31B buses every hr from Lower Abbey St, Dublin. Journey time: 1 hr.* DART *from Connolly/Pearse stations, every 15/20 mins. Journey time: 20 mins.*

Kilcullen, *45 km (28 miles) SW of Dublin.* Abbey with interesting sculptured effigies, remains of residence of medieval Leinster kings on summit of Knockaulin hill. Hide Out bar at village crossroads has arm of Dan Donnelly, early 19th c prizefighter, in glass case. Keep an eye on it over lunch. Attractive Liffeyside walk. *Bus from Busaras, Dublin, four buses daily. Journey time: 1 hr.*

Kildare, *54 km (33 miles) W of Dublin.* St Brigid's Cathedral (CI) and round tower, Japanese Gardens (*see* PARKS AND GARDENS), Irish National Stud and Irish Horse Museum (*see* MUSEUMS). *Bus from Busaras, Dublin. Journey time: 1 hr. Frequent train from Heuston station, Dublin.*

Lucan, *16 km (10 miles) W of Dublin.* Small, attractive village with central green. Walks along towpath of nearby Grand Canal, also fishing. Spectacular views of River Liffey. *25, 66, 66A, 67 buses every 30 mins from Dublin. Journey time: 45 mins.*

Lusk, *24 km (15 miles) NE of Dublin.* Market gardening town with interesting round tower and ancient church. Lusk Heritage Centre (*see* MUSEUMS). *3 km (2 miles)* E is small seaside village of Rush. *33 bus from Dublin every hr. Journey time: 1 hr.*

Malahide, *16 km (10 miles) N of Dublin.* Seaside town set on estuary, with a huge new marina. Good shopping, wide range of walks along coast road. Malahide Castle and Fry model railway (*see* HISTORICAL PLACES). *32A, 32A, 42, 102, 230 buses from Dublin every 45 mins. Journey time: 45 mins. Also train.*

Maynooth, *24 km (15 miles) W of Dublin.* Small, attractive university town set beside Royal Canal, *St Patrick's College* has chapel, library, sacristy, museum (*see* MUSEUMS). College and grounds, mid-June–mid-Sept. ☎ *628 5222. Maynooth Castle,* near college gates, 12th c ruins. *Key at college. Carton House* at E end of town is imposing mid-18th c mansion, in process of being taken over by the State. Check Dublin TIO for opening times. *66, 67A buses from Dublin every 20 mins. Journey time: 50 mins. Train from Connolly station, Dublin. Journey time: 30 mins.*

Monkstown, *10 km (6 miles) SW of Dublin.* Seaside suburb between Blackrock and Dun Laoghaire. *Comhaltas Ceoltóiri Éireann, 32 Belgrave Sq:* cultural institute, Irish music museum. Basement turned into Irish country kitchen; open fire, flagstone floor provide a great atmosphere for regular Irish music sessions, ☎ *280 0295. Lambert Puppet Theatre and Museum, Clifton Lane:* highly entertaining shows, Ireland's only puppet museum, ☎ *280 0974. 7, 7A, 8 bus from Dublin every 10 mins. Journey time: 40 mins.* DART *to Monkstown.*

Mosney, *40 km (25 miles) N of Dublin.* Holiday centre with indoor and outdoor facilities, including amusement park, computer facilities, horse riding, swimming. Audio-visual presentation on Boyne Valley history. Fine adjacent beach. *Open to day visitors, May–Sept,* ☎ *(041) 36441. Trains from Connolly station, Dublin, every 2 hrs in summer. Journey time: 1 hr.*

Newbridge House and Demesne, *Donabate, 0.8 km (0.5 mile) N of Swords.* 18th c mansion with original furnishings; drawing room is one of Ireland's best Georgian interiors. Kitchen has many period utensils. In courtyard, old coaches, also carpenter's workshop, coachhouse, dairy and other outbuildings. Many farm animals. Café, picnic area. Beyond walled garden with fruit trees, rolling parkland. *Apr–Sept, Tues–Fri, 10 a.m.–5 p.m. Sat, 11 a.m.–6 p.m. Sun, BH, 2 p.m.–6 p.m. Nov–Mar, Sat, Sun, BH, 2 p.m.–6 p.m.* ☎ *843 6534. Frequent trains from Connolly station. Journey time: 30 mins. Connecting bus from station.*

Newgrange, *11 km (7 miles) W of Drogheda.* Newgrange and Dowth prehistoric tombs, *open all year.* ☎ *041 24274.*

Newtownmountkennedy, *Co Wicklow, 34 km (21 miles) S of*

Dublin. Small, attractive village, walk up hill past St Matthew's Church (CI), built 1789.

Peatland World, *Lullymore, Co Kildare (on R414, near Allen-wood)*. Fascinating centre shows the history and development of Ireland's bogs. Includes many old photographs, old machinery, details of flora and fauna, reconstructions of rooms from a traditional turf worker's cottage. Video. ☎ *(045) 60133.*

Portmarnock, *24 km (15 miles) NE of Dublin*. 5 km (3 miles) long sandy beach. Coastal walks. *32, 32A buses from Dublin every 30 mins. Journey time: 1 hr. Train from Connolly station every 2 hrs. Journey time: 25 mins.*

Roundwood, *40 km (25 miles) S of Dublin*. Ireland's highest village, *238 km (780 ft)* above sea level. The Main Street is virtually the village. Boats may be hired on nearby reservoir. Nearby loughs Dan and Tay. Roundwood Inn has good pub grub, restaurant. St Kevin's private bus service, twice daily to and from St Stephen's Green, Dublin. ☎ *281 8119. Journey time: 1½ hrs.*

Sandycove, *13 km (8 miles) SE of Dublin*. James Joyce tower (*see* HISTORIC PLACES). Forty Foot bathing place is male only, but sometimes brave women defy the elements. *8 bus from Dublin, every 20 mins. Journey time: 45 mins. Also* DART *to Sandycove.*

Skerries, *30 km (19 miles) N of Dublin*. Pleasant holiday resort and fishing town; walks along harbour and seafront. Shenick's Island, just offshore, can be reached on foot at low tide. *33, 41, 41B, 230 buses from Lower Abbey St, Dublin, every hr. Journey time: 1¼ hrs. Frequent train from Connolly station, every 2 hrs. Journey time: 50 mins.*

Slane, *47 km (29 miles) N of Dublin*. Small, tree-lined village. Ledwidge museum (*see* MUSEUMS). Nearby Slane Hill associated with St Patrick; remains of 16th c church, school. Fine views of Boyne Valley from Trim to Drogheda. *Bus 3 times daily from Dublin. Journey time: 45 mins. Bus four times daily from Drogheda. Journey time: 20 mins.*

Swords, *16 km (10 miles) N of Dublin*. Pleasant small town set on Dublin—Belfast road. Castle (*see* ANCIENT MONUMENTS), round tower (*see* ANCIENT MONUMENTS) and museum (*see* MUSEUMS).

Nearby estuary. *33, 41, 41B, 230 buses every 20 mins from Eden Quay, Dublin. Journey time: 50 mins.*

Trim, *45 km (28 miles) NW of Dublin.* Rich in history. Impressive ruins of castle built in late 12th c, largest Anglo-Irish fortress in country. Now a heritage town, a new folk theatre has been complemented by a heritage, cultural and genealogical centre. Town Hall, Castle St, has records dating from 1659, ☎ *31238. Bus from Busarus, Dublin, four times daily. Journey time: 1 hr.*

PARKS AND GARDENS

Modern Dublin may be heavily built up, but it still has many oases of green space. The Phoenix Park is Europe's largest and includes Dublin Zoo. Other major parks include Marlay, the National Botanic Gardens and St Stephen's Green.

Ardgillen Demesne, *near Skerries, 27 km (17 miles) N of Dublin.* A fine expanse of rolling parkland, 78 ha (194 acres): sanctuary for many species of mammals and bird. Restored castle, sea views.

Ashford, *Co Wicklow, 40 km (25 miles) S of Dublin.* Mount Usher gardens have marvellous variety of plants in very natural setting beside the River Vartry. Waterfalls, pets' cemetery. Shops, tearoom. *Mid Mar—Nov 30, Mon—Sat, 10.30 a.m.—6 p.m. Sun, 11 a.m.—6 p.m.* ☎ *(0404) 40116. Bus from Busarus, Dublin, every 2 hrs. Journey time: 1¼ hrs.*

Ayesha Castle, *Victoria Rd, Killiney.* 19th c Victorian Castle with exotic gardens and woodland. Tea-room, craft shop. ☎ *285 2323.*

Bushy Park. Attractive S Dublin park runs from Templeogue to banks of River Dodder. *49, 49A buses from Crampton Quay.*

Dublin Literary Park, *St Patrick's Park, Dublin 8.* Adjacent to St Patrick's Cathedral the park commemorates Dublin's many literary figures, from Wilde and Yeats to Joyce and Beckett.

Dublin Zoo, *Phoenix Park.* One of Europe's finest, with many species of animals, birds and reptiles from all over the world, in modern houses and outdoor enclosures. Landscaping with flowering shrubs and trees adds to the beauty of the location. Considerable plans for expansion. Restaurant. ☎ *677 1425. All year,* *daily, 9.30 a.m. — sunset. 10, 25, 26 buses from city centre.*

Fairview Park, *Fairview, Dublin 3.* Not the most scenic setting, in a semi-industrialised area of N Dublin, but plenty of green space. *20A, 20B, 30, 44A buses from city centre to Fairview.*

Fernhill Gardens, *Sandyford, Co Dublin.* Parkland, woodland, rocky and water gardens, dating back over 200 years. *Mar — Nov, Tues — Sat, BH, 11 a.m. — 5 p.m. Sun, 2 p.m. — 6 p.m.* ☎ *295 6000.*

Garden of Remembrance, *Parnell Sq, Dublin 1.* Pool, dominated by sculpture of Children of Lir, is dedicated to all who died for Irish freedom. *May — Sept, daily, 9.30 a.m. — 8 p.m. Mar, Apr, Oct, 11 a.m. — 7 p.m. Nov — Feb, 11 a.m. — 4 p.m.*

Herbert Park, *Ballsbridge, Dublin 4.* Small, attractively laid-out park with large lake and impressive flower displays. Tennis courts. *5, 7, 8, 45 buses to US Embassy, 10, 46A buses to Morehampton Rd.*

Howth Castle Gardens, *Howth, Co Dublin.* Magnificent rhodo-dendron gardens in steeply sloping setting. Best seen in May/early June. ☎ *832 2624. All year, 8 a.m. — sunset. 31 bus every hr from Lower Abbey St, Dublin. Journey time: 1 hr.* DART *from Connolly/Pearse stations, every 15 — 20 mins. Journey time: 20 mins.*

Japanese Gardens, *Kildare.* Exquisite layout symbolises the life of man; gardens are the finest of their kind in Ireland. *17 Mar — Oct, daily, 9.30 a.m. — 6 p.m.* ☎ *(045) 21617. Bus from Busarus. Journey time: 1 hr.*

Marlay Park, *Rathfarnham, Dublin 16.* Extensive park with nature trail, woodlands, large pond. Wicklow Way walk starts here. Model steam railway. Fine restored house. Stable courtyard has remarkable collection of craft workshops. *Daily, 10 a.m. — 5 p.m. 47B bus from city centre.*

Merrion Square, *Dublin 2.* Neatly kept park has only been opened to the public in recent years. Framed by the well-preserved houses on surrounding three sides. Fourth side is partly occupied by National Gallery of Ireland.

Millenium Park, *City Hall, Dublin 2.* Small park is oasis in heart of the city.

National Botanic Gardens, *Botanic Rd, Glasnevin, Dublin 9.* Extensive selection of trees, flowering shrubs and tropical plants. Ambitious project has restored main 19th c glasshouse. Fine walks in gardens and along adjacent bank of River Tolka. ☎ *837 4388. Summer, Mon−Sat, 9 a.m.−6 p.m. Sun, 11 a.m.−5 p.m. Winter, Mon−Sat, 10 a.m.−4.30 p.m. Sun, 11 a.m.−4.30 p.m. 13, 19, 34 buses from city centre to Botanic Rd.*

North Bull Island. 5 km (3 mile) long sandy island offshore from N Dublin, reached by causeway from main coast road at Dollymount. *30 bus from city centre to causeway, then 0.8 km (0.5 mile) walk to island.*

Palmerstown Park, *Dublin 6.* Pleasant green space in South Dublin suburb.

Phoenix Park. Largest park in Europe, 709 ha (1,752 acres) has many tree-lined roads, several lakes and herds of deer. Cycling paths, also horse-drawn transport through the park. Heritage Trail. Furry Glen nature tail in NW of park has many interesting trees and plants. From the Fifteen Acres, you will see many of Dublin's landmarks. Ashtown Castle is a restored 17th c castle with a visitor centre detailing history of the park. *25, 26 buses from city centre to Parkgate St entrance; 10 bus from city centre to North Circular Rd entrance.*

Powerscourt Gardens and Waterfall, *Enniskerry.* Gardens were laid out in the 19th c in the grand Italian style, complete with terraces and lake. Also a Japanese-style garden. Magnificent views to Sugar Loaf Mountain; gardens regarded as some of the finest in Europe, with vistas to match. At end of the estate is the impressive Powerscourt Waterfall. *Summer, daily, 9.30 a.m.−5.30 p.m.* ☎ *286 7676. 44 bus from Dublin every 1½ hrs. Journey time: 1½ hrs.* DART *to Bray, then 85 bus to Enniskerry.*

Ranelagh Gardens Park, *Ranelagh Rd, Dublin 6.* Small new park with lake, alongside defunct Harcourt St−Bray railway line. On site of Ireland's first hot-air balloon ascent in 1785. *44, 48A, 62, 86 buses from city centre to Ranelagh Rd.*

Sandymount Strand, *Sandymount, Dublin 4.* When tide is out, large expanse of sand provides plenty of space for walks and fresh sea air, with good views of Howth across Dublin Bay. When the tide is in, use the seashore path which stretches for just over 0.8 km (0.5 mile) between road and beach. *3 bus from city centre to Sandymount tower.*

St Anne's Park, *Mount Prospect Ave, Clontarf, Dublin 3.* Attractive park has rose garden which is full of colour in summer. Most of the park consists of woodland, with lake. Follow the path for a really rural walk only 5 km (3 mile) from city centre. *30, 44A buses from city centre.* DART *from city centre to Killester, 800 m.*

St Enda's Park, *Rathfarnham, Dublin 14.* 10 ha (25 acres) of delightful park with ornamental lake, woodland and walled garden. See nearby Pearse museum. *Daily, 10 a.m. – 5 p.m. 16, 47B buses from city centre.*

St Stephen's Green, *Dublin 2.* A city centre oasis at the top of Grafton St. Ideal for strolling, relaxing or simply observing the antics of one's fellow creatures. Large lake with waterfall, many well-kept flowerbeds. Garden for blind people with plants labelled in Braille. See Henry Moore's sculptured tribute to W. B. Yeats and Edward Delaney's memorial to Wolfe Tone. *All year, Mon – Sat, 8 a.m. – dusk. Sun, 10 a.m. – dusk. Horse-drawn carriage trips start from the Grafton St corner of the Green.*

Tymon Park, *Tallaght/Terenure, Dublin.* Dublin's newest large park, covering 300 ha (320 acres). Ornamental water feature, around 16 km (10 miles) of walkways. Extensive sports facilities in preparation. *65 bus from Crampton Quay (city centre) to Tallaght.*

Wolfe Tone Park, *Jervis St, Dublin 1.* City-centre park which was once an ancient burial ground. Tombstones still line the surrounding walls, but the inscriptions are too faded to be read.

PUBS

Since few writers who have lived in Dublin have not eulogised about the city's pubs at one time or another (frequently at length!) the same will not be attempted here. However, there are some 900 Dublin pubs, and you are unlikely to visit the city without becoming acquainted with, and probably acquiring an affection for, at least a few of them.

Some are in suburban locations, with somewhat dull modern designs, and some are renovated pubs, liberally decorated with 'ancient' plastic panels and fake 'antique' mirrors. Thankfully, however, the trend towards modernising and 'improving' pubs seems to have passed its peak and many genuinely ancient pubs, full of atmosphere and character, still exist. Most are in the city-centre area, and a good, selective cross-section is listed here.

Opening hours: Mon – Sat, 10.30 a.m. – 11 p.m. Sun, 11 a.m. – 11 p.m. In summer, evening closing times are extended by 30 mins. Also 30 mins 'drinking up' time after closing. Pubs are not obliged to be open during these hours and some, particularly suburban pubs, may close at slack times during the day.

Abbey Tavern, *Howth.* Old-world charm, authenticity and simplicity, with blazing turf fires, original stone walls, flagged floors and gas lights. Parts of the inn date back to 15th c when it was built as a seminary for local monks. Restaurant, entertainment. *31, 31B buses from Dublin city centre.* DART to Howth.

Bowes, *31 Fleet St, Dublin 2.* Opposite back door of *The Irish Times* offices, this old-world pub with its traditional decor is a favourite drinking spot for journalists from that paper. Plenty of atmosphere, often packed.

Brazen Head, *Bridge St, Dublin 8.* A pub may have been on this site since 13th c. Full of character and atmosphere, comparatively little changed over the years. Robert Emmet said to have planned his 1803 rebellion here; his desk and chair are on view. *21A, 78A, 123 buses to Cornmarket.*

Brian Boru, *Glasnevin, Dublin 9.* Pub has changed comparatively little since its 1894 foundation. Said to be only pub in Ireland with cross over main entrance door. *13, 19, 34 bus from city centre to Glasnevin.*

Byrne's, *Galloping Green, Stillorgan, Co Dublin.* Touch of the quiet country pub about this establishment on the Stillorgan Rd, with its wood panelling and photographs of bygone sporting achievements. *46A bus from city centre.*

Café en Seine, *40 Dawson St, Dublin 2.* Lively, authentic repro of a typical Parisian pub.

Connolly's The Sheds, *Clontarf Rd.* One of the district's last 'unimproved' pubs has old-world atmosphere and fascinating historical photographs of the area. *30 bus.*

Conways, *Parnell St, Dublin 1.* Probably Dublin's second oldest pub, founded in 1745, the same year as the Rotunda Hospital across the road. Popular with medical and theatrical people.

Davy Byrne's, *Duke St, Dublin 2.* Once the 'moral pub' where Leopold Bloom dined on gorgonzola and burgundy on Bloomsday, 16 June 1904. Spit and sawdust has long since gone; interior is refined for modern times, although you can still see the bacchanalian murals executed by Cecil Salkeld, Brendan Behan's father-in-law.

Dockers, *5 Sir John Rogerson's Quay, Dublin 2.* Trendy riverside pub often frequented by artists from nearby recording studios. Lounge bar, snug and darts room, also sing-songs around the piano.

Doheny & Nesbitt, *5 Lower Baggot St, Dublin 2.* Traditional darkwood pub, little changed this century. Renowned for its snugs. Also upstairs lounge. Journalists, politicians and TV personalities frequent the establishment.

Dubliner's Bar, *Jury's Hotel, Ballsbridge, Dublin 4.* One of the city's best bars, furnished like an old-style living room where you can take your ease on settees or armchairs. Century-old printing press borrowed from the *Wexford People* newspaper; old photographs and press cuttings on walls are historically interesting and often highly amusing. *5, 7, 8, 45 buses from city centre.* DART *to Lansdowne Rd station, 100 metres.*

The Duke, *Duke St, Dublin 2.* Small, homely pub, between Dawson St and Grafton St, with renovated interior and friendly welcome.

Grogan's Castle Lounge, *15 South William St.* Facing the Powerscourt Centre, one of Dublin's best-known literary and cultural pubs.

Harry Byrne's, *107 Howth Rd, Dublin 3.* Traditional old-style family-run pub, with friendly atmosphere. Beer garden in summer. *30 bus to Howth Rd.*

Hill 16, *28 Middle Gardiner St, Dublin 1.* Fascinating city centre pub with many sporting connections.

Horse Shoe Bar, *Shelbourne Hotel, St Stephen's Green, Dublin 2.* Despite refurbishing, this bar, beloved of literary and sporting types in Dublin, retains much of its atmosphere. Good place to bump into local and visiting celebrities.

Horse and Tram, *Eden Quay, Dublin 1.* Good, lively atmosphere. A favourite recreation spot for *Irish Press* journalists.

Joxer Daly's, *103-104 Upper Dorset St, Dublin 1.* Victorian-style pub with open fires and small snug.

Kielys, *22 Donnybrook Rd, Dublin 4.* Recently renovated pub with luxurious, plush style. Another favourite place for off-duty RTE people. *10, 46A buses to Donnybrook Rd.*

Kitty O'Shea's, *Grand Canal St Upper, Dublin 4.* Another trendy pub with pre-Raphaelite-style stained glass and hearty atmosphere, frequented by TV personalities and rugby fraternity. Pyke's cartoon portraits of some well-known customers adorn the walls. *5, 7, 8, 45 buses to Northumberland Rd, 400 metres.*

Leopardstown Inn, *Brewery Rd, Co Dublin.* Modern establishment has several bars, lively atmosphere. Facilities include nightclub. *46A, 86 buses from city centre.*

Long Hall, *51 South Great George's St, Dublin 2.* Dublin's most ornate traditional pub, all chandeliers, lamps, mirrors and ornate woodwork, dating back to late 19th c.

Madigans, *135 Morehampton Rd, Dublin 4.* Modern-style pub is favourite recreation spot for radio and TV people from RTE, just up the road. *10, 46A buses to Belmont Ave.*

Mother Redcap's Tavern, *Black Lane, Dublin 8.* An 18th c tavern stood near this site; recreation using materials from an old country flour mill is as authentic as possible. *21A, 23, 78A buses to High St.*

Mulligan's, *Poolbeg St, Dublin 2.* One of Dublin's most famous pubs, immortalised by James Joyce. Interior is dark and thankfully unmodernised, full of character and characters.

Neary's, *Chatham St, Dublin 2.* Ornate, Victorian-style pub just off Grafton St, oozing brass, mahogany and literary characters. Once a favourite lounging place of poet Patrick Kavanagh.

O'Brien's, *Sussex Terrace, Dublin 4.* Charming old-style pub, complete with dark snugs and lively conversation. Decor has changed little in 50 years. A traditional 'gem' just yards from Burlington Hotel. *11, 11A, 13, 46A buses from city centre to Upper Leeson St.*

O'Connell's, *South Richmond St, Dublin 2.* Real old-style Dublin bar, complete with red plush seats. Plenty of 'gutsy' atmosphere, little changed in last 30 years.

O'Donoghues, *15 Merrion Row, Dublin 2.* Traditional music pub frequented by many musicians, most notably members of the Dubliners. Interesting portraits; very lively, especially after dark.

O'Neill's, *Pearse St, Dublin 2.* Lively establishment between city centre and Pearse station, Westland Row. Enlivened even further with plentiful hanging plants and antique mirrors.

O'Shea's, *Clonskeagh Rd, Dublin 6.* Renovated pub with good atmosphere and interesting poster selection. *11, 62 buses to Clonskeagh Rd.*

Old Chinaman, *Ship St, Dublin 8.* New pub on site of early 19th c establishment, just below Dublin Castle, has photographs of old pub and the Liberties in historic times. *21A, 50, 50A, 54, 54A, 78A, 123 buses from city centre to Christchurch Place.*

Old Stand, *37 Exchequer St, Dublin 2.* A very 'sporting' pub, favoured by horse-racing and rugby people.

Oval, *Middle Abbey St, Dublin 1.* Often used by journalists from nearby Independent Newspapers. Upstairs lounge, with caricatures of some noted journalistic customers, has more atmosphere than downstairs bar.

Palace Bar, *Fleet St, Dublin 2.* Genuine, old-time Dublin pub, untouched by renovators. Tiled floor, dark panelling, mirrors, leaded glass in entrance doors. Interesting photographs and cartoons of some of its noted literary patrons. Back bar and upstairs lounge also worth sampling.

Porto Bello, *South Richmond St, Dublin 2.* Fascinating late 19th c bar little altered over the years. Original panelling, even bookshelf full of genuine antique books and vintage wireless set. Across the street is early 19th c canal hotel, tastefully refurbished into College.

Ryans, *Parkgate St, Dublin 7.* Marvellous traditional bar, complete with snugs and old-fashioned lamps. Remodelled in 1896 and little changed since. *25, 26, 51 buses from city centre.*

Scruffy Murphys, *Powers Court, off Mount St Lower, Dublin 2.* One of Dublin's most interesting refurbished pubs. Dark, low-ceilinged, full of character. First-floor restaurant. *5, 7, 8, 45, 84 buses from city centre to Mount St Lower.*

Sir Arthur Conan Doyle, *Doyle's Corner, Phibsboro', Dublin 7.* Old pub was renovated and refurbished some years ago. It now has an interesting neo-Victorian interior, one of Dublin's most pleasant 'modern' pubs. *19, 19A buses from city centre to Doyle's Corner.*

Smyth's, *Haddington Rd, Dublin 4.* 150-year-old pub with unchanged wainscoting and wooden ceilings. Old beer and whiskey mirrors. Convivial atmosphere. *10 bus to Upper Baggot St/ Haddington Rd junction.*

Stag's Head, *Dame Court, off Dame St, Dublin 2.* One of Dublin's oldest pubs, built in 1770 and remodelled in 1895. Plenty of historic atmosphere.

Toners, *Lower Baggot St, Dublin 2.* Ancient country-style pub in heart of city. Said to be over 200-years old, with shelves and drawers untouched for past century, once part of the grocery section of the pub. Old-world atmosphere complemented by stone floors.

PUB GRUB

The following selection of Dublin area pubs serve a good selection of 'pub grub', both snacks and meals, together with wine. Some of the pubs listed only serve meals at lunchtime; those serving evening food as well are marked with an asterisk. Prices are generally moderate.

Ashtons, *11 Vergemount, Dublin 6,* ☎ *269 8982.*
Barge Inn, *42 Charlemont St, Dublin 2,* ☎ *475 0005.*
Belcamp Inn, *Newtown Industrial Estate, Dublin 5,* ☎ *847 2061.*
Black Lion Inn, *207A Emmet Rd, Inchicore, Dublin 8,* ☎ *453 4580.*
Bowes, *31 Fleet St, Dublin 2,* ☎ *671 4038.*
Bruxelles, *Harry St (off Grafton St), Dublin 2,* ☎ *677 5362.*
Cusack Stand, *78 Lower Camden St, Dublin 2,* ☎ *675 3414.**
Davy Byrne's, *21 Duke St, Dublin 2,* ☎ *677 5217.*
Delgany Inn, *Delgany, Co Wicklow,* ☎ *287 5701.**
Dollymount House, *366 Clontarf Rd, Dublin 3,* ☎ *833 2701.**
Doran's, *90 Marlborough St, Dublin 1,* ☎ *874 0685.**
Doyle's, *9 College St, Dublin 1,* ☎ *671 0616.**
Duffy's, *Main St, Malahide, Co Dublin,* ☎ *845 0735.*
The Duke, *9 Duke St, Dublin 2,* ☎ *679 9553.*
Emmet House, *1 Vincent St, Inchicore, Dublin 8,* ☎ *453 3845.*
Foxes, *Glencullen, Co Dublin,* ☎ *295 5647.**
Gleesons, *Booterstown Ave, Booterstown, Co Dublin,* ☎ *288 0236.**
The Goat, *Goatstown, Dublin 14,* ☎ *498 3216.**
Halfway House, *Ashtown, Dublin 7,* ☎ *838 3218.*
Harry Byrne, *107 Howth Rd, Dublin 3,* ☎ *833 2650.*
Healys Black Lion House, *Clondalkin, Dublin 22,* ☎ *459 2091.*
Kitty O'Shea's, *23 Upper Grand Canal St, Dublin 4,* ☎ *660 9965.**
Leopardstown Inn, *Brewery Rd, Stillorgan, Co Dublin,* ☎ *288 9189.**
Lord Mayor's, *Main St, Swords, Co Dublin,* ☎ *840 7668.**
Madigan's, *135 Morehampton Rd, Donnybrook, Dublin 4,* ☎ *269 3527.*
McGraths, *22 Drumcondra Rd, Dublin 9,* ☎ *830 5309.*
Orchard Inns, *Butterfield Ave, Rathfarnham, Dublin 14,* ☎ *494 6705.* Stillorgan, Co Dublin,* ☎ *288 8470.*
Palmerstown House, *Palmerstown, Dublin 20,* ☎ *626 4505.**
Ryan's, *28 Parkgate St, Dublin 8,* ☎ *677 6097.**
Scruffy Murphy's, *1 Power's Court (off Lower Mount St), Dublin 2,* ☎ *676 6673.**

Searson's, *Upper Baggot St, Dublin 4,* ☎ *660 0494.* *
Spawell Lounge, *Wellington Lane, Templeogue, Dublin 12,* ☎ *490 1826.* *
Step Inn, *Stepaside, Co Dublin,* ☎ *295 6202.* *
Terenure House, *24 Terenure Rd North, Dublin 6,* ☎ *490 5686.*
Toner's, *139 Lower Baggot St, Dublin 2,* ☎ *676 3090.*
Wicklow Arms, *Delgany, Co Wicklow,* ☎ *287 4611.* *
Yellow House, *Rathfarnham, Dublin 14,* ☎ *493 1387.* *

RESTAURANTS

Dublin has a good variety of restaurants to suit most tastes and all pockets. They range from the incredibly expensive, where dinner for two is likely to cost well over £100, to modestly priced bistros and clean, homely establishments, where a meal can be had for around £5. Catering standards are much improved over the last few years. The long established restaurants, those that weathered the most recent recession, are usually worth trying. An increasing number of Dublin restaurants have ethnic menus from around the world, and at long last, there's a growing awareness of, and emphasis on, traditional Irish cuisine.

Bord Fáilte, the Irish Tourist Board, runs a special Tourist Menu scheme for lunch and dinner at selected restaurants. Otherwise, many restaurants offer bargain prices for dinner in the early evening, starting at around 6.30 p.m. Bord Fáilte also publishes a diner's guide, listing many restaurants in Dublin and elsewhere in the Republic. The following restaurants have been grouped into three categories, expensive (£££) £15 per person and over, medium (££) £7.50 to £15 per person and inexpensive (£) below £7.50. Prices exclude drinks.

£££
Ayumi-Ya, *Newpark Centre, Blackrock, Co Dublin,* ☎ *283 1767.*
Authentic Japanese cooking. Also **Ayumi-Ya Japanese Steakhouse,** *132 Lr Baggot St, Dublin 2,* ☎ *662 0233.*
Beaufield Mews, *Woodlands Ave, Stillorgan, Co Dublin,* ☎ *288*

0375. Coach house restaurant accompanies antiques shop. Homely, filling fare.

Berkeley Court, *Lansdowne Rd, Dublin 4,* ☎ *660 1711.* Berkeley Room's French cuisine is complemented by the Conservatory Grill.

Bon Appetit, *9 James Terrace, Malahide, Co Dublin,* ☎ *845 0314.* Gourmet restaurant with extensive wine list, beside the sea.

Café Caruso, *47 South William St, Dublin 2,* ☎ *677 0708.* Popular restaurant has lively atmosphere.

Court Hotel, *Killiney, Co Dublin,* ☎ *285 1622.* Two restaurants, the Island and the Library Grill, have wide choice of dishes.

Chandni, *174 Pembroke Rd, Dublin 4,* ☎ *668 1458.* Sophisticated Indian restaurant.

The Commons, *Newman House, 85-86 St Stephen's Green, Dublin 2,* ☎ *475 2597.* Luxuriously designed restaurant, enlivened by contemporary art, serving well balanced classic cooking.

Clarets, *63–65 Main St, Blackrock, Co Dublin,* ☎ *288 2008.* Specialises in fish and game in season.

Conrad, *Earlsfort Terrace, Dublin 2,* ☎ *676 5555.* Alexandra restaurant in this outstandingly run hotel is a dignified setting for Irish and Continental cuisine, while the Plurabelle Brasserie is more informal.

Coopers, *Lr Leeson St,* ☎ *676 8615. Greystones,* ☎ *287 3914, Kilternan,* ☎ *295 9349, Monkstown,* ☎ *284 2037.* Affordably priced international cuisine in pleasant surroundings.

Dobbins, *15 St Stephen's Lane (rear Upper Mount St), Dublin 2,* ☎ *676 4679.* Lively bistro atmosphere for lunch and dinner.

Ernies, *Mulberry Gardens (behind Kiely's pub), Donnybrook, Dublin 4,* ☎ *269 3300.* Rich, classical cuisine in an elegant, mannered setting.

Fitzpatrick's Killiney Castle Hotel, *Killiney, Co Dublin,* ☎ *284 0700.* Truffles restaurant, open for lunch and dinner, has seafood and game dishes.

Gresham, *O'Connell St, Dublin 1,* ☎ *874 6881.* Well-known hotel restaurant at Parnell Sq end of O'Connell St.

Grey Door, *23 Upper Pembroke St, Dublin 1,* ☎ *676 3286.*

Scandinavian and Russian cuisine. Basement Pier 32 is bistro-style restaurant.

Guinea Pig, *17 Railway Rd, Dalkey, Co Dublin,* ☎ *285 9055.* Gourmet restaurant provides fine eating in refined surroundings.

Jury's, *Ballsbridge, Dublin 4,* ☎ *660 5000.* Embassy Garden and Kish restaurant are upmarket, the latter specialising in fish, while the Coffee Dock provides almost round-the-clock grill type service.

Kapriol, *45 Lr Camden St, Dublin 2,* ☎ *475 1235.* Fantastic Italian cuisine and wine list, with prices to match.

King Sitric, *East Pier, Howth, Dublin 13,* ☎ *832 5235.* Excellent seafood restaurant, facing the harbour, with equally ambitious wine list.

Kingswood Country House, *Kingswood, Naas Rd, Dublin 22,* ☎ *459 2428.* Country house restaurant with homely cooking and matching atmosphere.

Le Coq Hardi, *15 Pembroke Rd, Dublin 4,* ☎ *668 4130.* French style restaurant with gourmet cooking, seasonal specialities and splendid cellar.

L'Ecrivain, *109 Lr Baggot St, Dublin 4,* ☎ *661 1919.* Traditional classic French cooking.

Little Lisbon, *2 Fownes St, Dublin 2 (beside Central Bank),* ☎ *671 1274.* Authentic Portuguese cuisine.

Lobster Pot, *9 Ballsbridge Terrace, Dublin 4,* ☎ *668 0025.* Gourmet seafood cooking complemented by extensive wine list.

Locks, *1 Windsor Terrace, Portobello, Dublin 8,* ☎ *454 3391.* Pleasantly set beside the Grand Canal. French cuisine.

McGrattans, *Fitzwilliam Lane, off Lr Baggot St, Dublin 2,* ☎ *661 8808.* International cuisine complemented by authentic Irish dishes in elegant surroundings.

Oisin's Irish Restaurant, *31 Upper Camden St, Dublin 2,* ☎ *475 3433.* Acclaimed servings of traditional Irish dishes, very expensive.

Old Dublin, *91 Francis St, Dublin 8,* ☎ *454 2028.* Scandinavian and Russian dishes with emphasis on fish. Comfortable atmosphere.

Old Schoolhouse, *Coolbanagher, Swords, Co Dublin,* ☎ *840 2846.* Bistro atmosphere in this former schoolhouse turned into well-appointed restaurant.

Parkers, *29 Pembroke Rd, Dublin 4,* ☎ *660 6140.* In basement of Lansdowne Hotel, this classy restaurant serves a wide-ranging international cuisine.

Patrick Guilbaud, *46 James Place, Lr Baggot St, Dublin 2 (behind Bank of Ireland headquarters),* ☎ *676 4192.* Fresh Irish ingredients used to create classical-style gourmet French dishes.

Rajdoot Tandoori, *26-28 Clarendon St, Dublin 2,* ☎ *679 4274.* North Indian cuisine, recommended for its vegetarian and curry dishes.

Red Bank, *7 Church St, Skerries, Co Dublin,* ☎ *849 1005.* Expensive but acclaimed seafood restaurant; the fish are landed at the nearby pier.

Restaurant na Mara, *Dun Laoghaire, Co Dublin,* ☎ *280 6797.* Elegant setting near the harbour for specialised and expensive seafood restaurant.

Roly's, *7 Ballsbridge Terrace, Dublin 4,* ☎ *668 2611.* Very popular bistro-type restaurant for lunch and dinner.

Roundwood Inn, *Roundwood, Co Wicklow,* ☎ *281 8107.* 17th c inn has gourmet restaurant and less expensive food in the bar.

Señor Sassis, *146 Upper Leeson St, Dublin 4,* ☎ *668 4544.* Popular restaurant serving Mediterranean-style cooking.

Terrace Café, *Temple Bar Hotel, Fleet St, Dublin 2,* ☎ *677 3333.* Spacious, modern restaurant with wide all day menu choice.

The Bistro Restaurant, *16-17 Lr Leeson St, Dublin 2,* ☎ *661 0585.* Intimate restaurant recommended for its cooking. Includes vegetarian dishes.

The Tea Room, *Clarence Hotel, Wellington Quay, Dublin 2,* ☎ *677 6178.* International menu in modern, conservatory style setting.

Tree of Idleness, *Seafront, Bray, Co Wicklow,* ☎ *286 3498.* Long established restaurant, full of ambience, modern and Greek Cypriot menus.

QV2, *15 St Andrew St, Dublin 2,* ☎ *677 3363.* Modern restaurant, with understated decor, always lively, serving international dishes.

££

Batz, *10 Baggot Lane, Ballsbridge, Dublin 4,* ☎ *660 0363.* Bright, comfortable restaurant serving wholesome food.

Break for the Border, *Johnson's Place, near Grafton St, Dublin 2,* ☎ *478 0300.* Extraordinary Mexican style decor, menu includes Tex-Mex dishes. Very lively spot.

Buttery Brasserie, *Royal Hibernian Way, Dublin 2,* ☎ *679 6259.* Food served at outdoor tables if weather fine.

Brahms & Liszt, *Swords Rd, Dublin 9,* ☎ *842 8383.* Varied menu, including vegetarian, handy place on way to airport.

Café Kylemore, *O'Connell St, Dublin 1,* ☎ *872 2138.* Café with Viennese style decor serving snacks and meals.

Captain America's, *Grafton Court, 44 Grafton St, Dublin 2,* ☎ *671 5266.* American-style food, including burgers.

Captain K's, *Dun Laoghaire shopping centre, Dun Laoghaire, Co Dublin,* ☎ *280 8119.* Typical American menu.

Clery's, *O'Connell St, Dublin 1,* ☎ *878 6000.* Self-service restaurant, tea room right in city centre.

Cora's, *1 St Mary's Rd, Ballsbridge, Dublin 4,* ☎ *660 0585.* It may have Formica topped tables, but it has a warm Italian welcome and food.

Courtyard, *Belmont Court, Belmont Ave, Donnybrook, Dublin 4,* ☎ *283 8815.* Lively spot for lunch and dinner, including vegetarian dishes.

Flanagan's Steakhouse, *61 O'Connell St, Dublin 1,* ☎ *873 1388.* Comfortable city centre surroundings, quick service.

FXB, *1A Lr Pembroke St, Dublin 2,* ☎ *676 4606, 3 The Crescent, Monkstown, Co Dublin,* ☎ *284 6187.* Cosy restaurants with good menu choice, including steaks.

Footplate Brasserie, *Heuston Station, Dublin 8,* ☎ *677 0287.* Unlikely setting for an excellent restaurant, with imaginative menus and interesting decor. All day à la carte.

Gallagher's Boxty House, *20-21 Temple Bar, Dublin 2,* ☎ *677 2762.* Authentic Irish cuisine for lunch and dinner.

Howth Lodge Hotel, *Howth, Dublin 13,* ☎ *832 1010.* Fine setting near Howth harbour. Lunchtime food in bar, also restaurant for more formal dinner.

Kilkenny Kitchen, *Nassau St, Dublin 2,* ☎ *677 7066.* Wide-ranging daytime menu, including lunch, but always busy.

Kingsland, *24 Castle St, Dalkey, Co Dublin,* ☎ *285 0647.* Excellent Chinese restaurant with ambience and a warm welcome.

Latchford's, *100 Lr Baggot St, Dublin 2,* ☎ *676 0784.* Recently renovated bistro-type restaurant with good menu choices. Also has accommodation.

La Cave, *South Anne St, Dublin 2,* ☎ *679 4409.* Excellent basement spot; you could well imagine yourself somewhere on the Left Bank.

Le Coquillage, *Westbury Mall, Dublin 2,* ☎ *679 5656, Blackrock shopping centre,* ☎ *288 3470.* Stylishly decorated, pleasing but inexpensive menus.

Mitchells, *21 Kildare St, Dublin 2,* ☎ *668 0361.* Cellar bistro restaurant is always packed for lunch, so best to arrive early.

Mr Hung's Chinese Restaurant, *5A The Crescent, Monkstown, Co Dublin,* ☎ *284 3365.* Fine decor and food.

National Gallery, *Merrion Sq, Dublin 2,* ☎ *668 6481.* **Fitzers** serves the gastronomic delights here, as it does in its own restaurants at *Dawson St* (☎ *677 1155), Upper Baggot St* (☎ *660 0644), The Point, North Wall* (☎ *874 3971),* and RDS, *Ballsbridge* (☎ *667 1301).*

Paddy Kavanagh, *Pembroke Row, Dublin 2,* ☎ *676 5056.* Informal bistro setting.

Pasta Fresca, *3-4 Chatham St, Dublin 2,* ☎ *679 2402.* Fresh pasta in authentic Italian menus.

Roche's Bistro, *12 New St, Malahide, Co Dublin,* ☎ *845 2777.* Cosy atmosphere, good cooking for lunch and dinner.

Runner Bean, *4 Nassau St, Dublin 2,* ☎ *679 4833.* Salads, quiches and other tempting dishes at this lunch-time venue.

£

Abrakebabra, *Lr Baggot St, Upper Baggot St, Blanchardstown, Bray, Clondalkin, Crumlin, Donnybrook, Dun Laoghaire, Fairview, Finglas, Kelly's Corner, Northside shopping centre, O'Connell St, Phibsboro', The Point, Rathmines, Rathfarnham, South Anne St, Tallaght, Westmoreland St.* Fast food chain.

Arnott's, *12 Henry St, Dublin 1,* ☎ *872 1111.* Department store self-service restaurant.

Beshoffs, *14 Westmoreland St, Dublin 2,* ☎ *677 8026.* Excellent fish and chips. Also *Upper O'Connell St.*

Bewley's, *Westmoreland St, South Great George's St, Grafton St, Mary St, Dundrum shopping centre, Stillorgan shopping centre, The Square shopping centre, Tallaght.* Variety of mainly inexpensive snacks and meals in interesting city centre locations, also suburban shopping centres.

Borza's, *Sandymount Green, Dublin 4,* ☎ *269 4130.* Excellent take-away. The Borza family name is certainly widespread in the Dublin take-away business.

Burdock's, *Werburgh St, Dublin 8 (near Christchurch Cathedral),* ☎ *545 0306.* Scrumptious fish and chips.

Burger King, *9 O'Connell St, 39 Grafton St, 15 Upper George's St, Dun Laoghaire, The Square shopping centre, Tallaght.* Burger restaurants.

Cafollas, *75 Mespil Rd, Dublin 4,* ☎ *660 3127.* Take-away and sit-down meals that are decidedly tasty.

Eddie Rocket's City Diner, *Blackrock, Donnybrook, Phibsboro', Rathmines, The Square, Tallaght.* Popular chain of fast food outlets.

Jonathan's Restaurant, *Irish Life Mall, Talbot St, Dublin 1,* ☎ *872 7528,* **Jonathan's Coffee Shop,** ILAC *centre, Moore St, Dublin 1,* ☎ *872 8313.*

McDonald's, *Artane Castle, Dublin 5, Belgard Rd, Tallaght, Roche's shopping centre, Blackrock, Donaghmede shopping centre, Upper George's St, Dun Laoghaire, 9 Grafton St, Kylemore Rd/Naas Rd corner, Nutgrove shopping centre, Rathfarnham, Upper O'Connell St, The Square, Tallaght, Swan* *shopping centre, Rathmines.* No introduction needed for this world-famous name in fast foods.

Pronto, *65A Ranelagh, Dublin 6,* ☎ *497 4174.* Plain grill-type fare in cosy surroundings.

Supermac, *Lr O'Connell St, Dublin 1,* ☎ *872 1828.* Yet another name on the ever-expanding fast food list in Dublin.

Winding Stair, *40 Lower Ormond Quay, Dublin 1,* ☎ *873 3292.* Café in bookshop, overlooking River Liffey.

SHOPPING

Dublin has an immense wealth of shopping, everything from the most luxurious fashion lines (with prices to match) to crafts. The main shopping areas are all within easy walking distance: Grafton St, Wicklow St, O'Connell St and Henry St. The Powerscourt Town House in South William St has a large assortment of shops, boutiques, restaurants and a craft centre all within a carefully restored 18th c mansion. There are more shopping complexes in the ILAC centre off Henry St, Creation Arcade, Grafton St, and the Irish Life Centre, Talbot St. The principal department stores are Clery's (O'Connell St), Brown Thomas's (Grafton St), Arnott's, Dunne's and Roche's (Henry St), and Habitat (St Stephen's Green).

SPECIALITIES
Antiques. Francis St is the main location for antique shops but also try Duke St, Lower Richmond St (Portobello), quays upstream from O'Connell Bridge, South Anne St.

Books. Clare St (Greene's), College Green (Books Upstairs), Dawson St (Hodges Figgis, Waterstone's), Nassau St (Fred Hanna's), St Stephen's Green (Hughes & Hughes).

Crafts. Dawson St (Fergus Farrell), Nassau St (Blarney Woollen Mills, Kilkenny Design Centre), Ormond Quay (Dublin Woollen Mills), Powerscourt Town House Centre, Tower Centre. All contain wide selection of Irish-made items, including clothes, tweed, lace, china, glassware, jewellery, etc.

Fashion. Grafton St (Brown Thomas, Next, Principles, etc), Henry St (Arnott's etc), Powerscourt Town House Centre (boutiques). Men's outfitters: Grafton St (Tricot Marine), Nassau St (Kennedy & McSharry, Kevin & Howlin).

Food and Wine. Clarendon St, off Grafton St (Magill's delicatessen), Donnybrook (O'Brien's wines), Duke St (Graham O'Sullivan), Grafton St (Bewleys, Marks & Spencer), Kildare St (Mitchell's wine merchants), Powerscourt Town House Centre (food and delicatessen shops), Westmoreland St (Bewley's). For 24-hr grocery shopping, Spar shops at Rathmines, Sandymount and Upper Baggot St.

MARKETS

Ashford. *Market every Mon p.m.*

Blackberry Market. *Rathmines, weekends. 14, 14A, 15A, 15B, 83 buses.*

Blackrock. *Sat (all day), Sun p.m. 7, 8, 45 buses from city centre,* DART.

Dun Laoghaire Harbour Market. *Sat, Sun (all day). 7, 8 buses from city centre to Dun Laoghaire.* DART.

Fish, Fruit and Vegetable Market. *Dublin 7.* Tremendous selection, plus jovial banter. *Mon—Fri, 8 a.m.—5 p.m. Tues, closes at 4 p.m. Sat, 8 a.m.—11 a.m. 34, bus from city centre to Church St.*

Iveagh. *Francis St (Liberties), Tues—Sat. 21A 78A, 123 buses from city centre to Thomas St.*

Mother Redcap's Market. *Back Lane,* Arts and Crafts, *daily. 21A, 78A buses to High St.*

Meath St/Thomas St. *Fri, Sat, 21A, 78A, 123 buses from city centre to Thomas St.*

Moore St. Mainly fruit and vegetbles. *Mon—Sat.*

Roundwood. Home-produce market featuring fresh foods and other lines, all from locality. Spectacular natural setting. *Sun p.m. St Kevin's private bus service from Dublin.* ☎ *281 8119.*

SHOPPING CENTRES

Blackrock. Very stylish, award-winning centre with many shops, including Roche's Stores, bookshop, fashion and shoes. *5, 7, 8 buses from city centre to Blackrock.* DART.

Dun Laoghaire Shopping Centre. Multi-level shopping centre with good selection of outlets. Outstanding views to Dun Laoghaire Harbour from top level pub/restaurant. *7, 8 buses from city centre to Dun Laoghaire.* DART.

ILAC Centre, *Talbot St, Dublin 1.* Good selection of shops, some restaurants. Large car park.

Irish Life Centre, *Moore St, Dublin 1.* Many general shops, some restaurants. High-tech library. Multi-storey car park.

Omni Park Shopping Centre, *Santry.* Ultra-modern centre, which includes 10-screen cinema.

Powerscourt Town House Centre, *South William St (off Grafton St), Dublin 2.* 1771 Georgian town house has been renovated into Dublin's most intriguing shopping centre. House with plasterwork and carvings meticulously restored; central area roofed over to form multi-level warren of shops. Many craft and other retail units, art gallery, restaurants. Even a resident pianist.

Royal Hibernian Way, *Dawson St, Dublin 2.* On site of old Royal Hibernian Hotel, once a coaching hotel. New centre features intimate street of 20 retail outlets, including chocolates and fashion.

Stillorgan Shopping Centre, *Stillorgan, Co Dublin.* Ireland's first shopping centre. Recently refurbished. Good variety of shops, Bewleys. *46A bus from city centre.*

St Stephen's Green Centre. One of Dublin's biggest shopping centres, containing 100 shops in impressively designed environment.

Tallaght Town Centre. The Square is a high-tech shopping complex, with 12-screen cinema.

Tower Centre, IDA *Enterprise Centre, Pearse St, Dublin 2.* Ireland's largest location for craft and design work, set in converted 19th c sugar refinery. Over 30 workshops; many types of traditional craftwork can be bought. *Mon−Fri, 9.30 a.m.−5.30 p.m. Sat, 10 a.m.−1 p.m. 1, 2, 3 buses from city centre.*

Westbury Centre, *off Grafton St, Dublin 2.* Small mall. Highlight is comprehensive Irish cheese shop.

VAT refunds: for visitors living outside Ireland, there are usually VAT refunds on purchases. Ask at point of purchase.

SPORT

Dublin has an amazing variety of sports on offer, covering even the most esoteric. Sports in the GAA code, such as **Gaelic football** and **hurling,** attract the biggest crowds to provincial and national finals. Full details of all GAA matches in the Dublin area from either local TIO or the Gaelic Athletic Association, Croke Park, Dublin 3, ☎ 836 3222. During the winter and spring, Dublin hosts many **rugby** matches, most notably internationals, which always draw big crowds to the city, making for entertaining and exhausting weekends. **Football** is widely played in Dublin, but provides less excitement than rugby; some international matches are held but many of the local competitions offer rather pedestrian spectator sport. Other outdoor sports such as **cricket** and **tennis**, are gaining in popularity. Private clubs, to which it may be possible to gain temporary membership, offer outstanding tennis facilities. More sedate sporting possibilities are offered at the **bowling** greens in most major parks. **Golf** is very popular, with some 40 courses in the Dublin area. Only one of these is not privately owned, but for most clubs, temporary visitor membership can be granted. Few other cities in Europe have such a fine collection of golf courses as Dublin. Tennis and squash are well-provided for. For more individualistic sports, such as **jogging, walking** and **cycling**, Dublin is an ideal venue. The city-centre streets, after business hours and at weekends, are ideal for running and jogging, while the mountains to the immediate south of Dublin are excellent territory for cycling, orienteering and walking.

The provision of indoor sports facilities such as **swimming,** has tended to lag behind developments in other European countries, but steps are being taken to improve matters. A national sports centre is planned for Dublin which, when completed, should be a welcome addition to the city's sports facilities.

BOWLING
Blackrock, *Green Rd, Blackrock,* ☎ *288 1933.*
Bray, *Failte Park, Bray,* ☎ *286 2527.*
Catholic Young Men's, *St Mary's Grounds, Terenure Rd North, Dublin 6,* ☎ *676 7571.*
Clontarf, *Malahide Rd, Donnycarney, Dublin 5,* ☎ *833 2669.*
Crumlin, *St Mary's Rd, Dublin 12,* ☎ *450 2417.*
Dun Laoghaire, *Moran Park, Dun Laoghaire,* ☎ *280 1179.*
Herbert Park, *Ballsbridge, Dublin 4,* ☎ *660 1875.*
Kenilworth, *Grosvenor Sq, Rathmines, Dublin 6,* ☎ *497 2305.*
Leinster, *Observatory Lane, Rathmines, Dublin 6,* ☎ *497 4673.*
Railway Union, *Park Ave, Sandymount, Dublin 4,* ☎ *269 1783.*
St James's Gate, *Iveagh Grounds, Crumlin Rd, Dublin 12,* ☎ *450 3597.*

BOWLING (indoor)
Dundrum Bowl, *Ballinteer Rd, Dublin 14,* ☎ *298 0909, 44, 48A buses from city centre to Dundrum.*
Stillorgan Bowl, *Stillorgan, Co Dublin,* ☎ *288 1656. 46A 62 buses from city centre to Stillorgan.*
Tallaght Sportsbowl, ☎ *459 9411.*
XL **Bowl,** *Palmerstown, Dublin 20,* ☎ *626 0700.*

CRICKET
Irish Cricket Union, *45 Foxrock Park, Foxrock, Dublin 18,* ☎ *289 3943* (home) ☎ *677 7504* (office). *Derek Scott, Secretary.*

GAA
Gaelic Athletic Association (details of matches), *Croke Park, Dublin 2,* ☎ *836 3222.*

GOLF COURSES
18 holes
Balbriggan, *Co Dublin,* ☎ *841 2173.*
Beaverstown, *Donabate, Co Dublin,* ☎ *843 4639.*
Beech Park, *Rathcoole, Co Dublin,* ☎ *458 0522.*
Castle, *Rathfarnham, Dublin 14,* ☎ *490 4207.*
Charlesland, *Greystones,* ☎ *287 6764.*
Clontarf, *Malahide Rd, Dublin 3,* ☎ *831 1305.*
Deerpark, *Howth, Co Dublin,* ☎ *832 2624.*
Donabate, *Co Dublin,* ☎ *843 6346.*
Dublin & County, *Corballis, Co Dublin,* ☎ *843 6228.*
Dun Laoghaire, *Co Dublin,* ☎ *280 1055.*
Edmondstown, *Rathfarnham, Dublin 14,* ☎ *493 2461.*
Elm Park, *Donnybrook, Dublin 4,* ☎ *269 3014.*
European, *Brittas Bay, Co Wicklow,* ☎ *0404 47415.*
Forrest Little, *Swords, Co Dublin,* ☎ *840 1183.*
Grange Park, *Rathfarnham, Dublin 16,* ☎ *493 2832.*
Hermitage, *Lucan, Co Dublin,* ☎ *626 4781.*
Howth, *Sutton, Dublin 13,* ☎ *832 3055.*
Island, *Donabate, Co Dublin,* ☎ *843 6205.*
Kildare Hotel and Country Club, *Straffan, Co Kildare,* ☎ *627 3333.*
Milltown, *Dublin 14,* ☎ *497 6090.*
Newlands, *Clondalkin, Dublin 22,* ☎ *459 3157/459 2903.*
Portmarnock, *Co Dublin,* (18 & 9 Holes) ☎ *832 3050.*
Royal Dublin, *Dollymount, Dublin 3,* ☎ *833 7153.*
Skerries, *Co Dublin,* ☎ *849 1204.*
Slade Valley, *Saggart, Co Dublin,* ☎ *458 2183.*
Stackstown, *Rathfarnham, Dublin 16,* ☎ *494 2338.*
St Margaret's, *near Dublin Airport,* ☎ *864 0400.*
Woodbrook, *Bray, Co Wicklow,* ☎ *282 4799.*

GREYHOUND RACING
Harold's Cross Stadium, *Harold's Cross Rd, Dublin 6.* Regular evening meetings, Feb–Dec. ☎ *497 1081. 16 bus from city centre.*

Shelbourne Park, *Ringsend, Dublin 4.* Regular evening meetings, Feb–Dec. ☎ *668 3502. 3 bus from city centre.*

HORSE RACING
Curragh, *48 km (30 miles) W of Dublin.* Set on the vast Curragh plain, all Ireland's classic races are held here. ☎ *(045) 41205. On race days, special buses from Busarus, Dublin and trains from Heuston station, Dublin.*
Fairyhouse, *26 km (16 miles) N of Dublin.* Attractive setting in Co Meath. ☎ *825 6167. On race days, special buses from Busarus, Dublin.*
Leopardstown, *Dublin 18.* Ultra-modern course with excellent facilities. Originally built in 1888 on lines of Sandown Park, but much modernised in recent years. ☎ *289 3607. 86 bus from city centre.*
Navan, *48 km (30 miles) NW of Dublin.* Rural setting in North Co Meath. ☎ *046 21350. Buses every 2 hrs from Busarus, Dublin. Journey time: 1 hr.*
Punchestown, *37 km (23 miles) SW of Dublin.* Fine racecourse near Naas. ☎ *045 97704. Special race day buses from Busarus, Dublin.*

ICE SKATING
Dublin Ice Rink, *Dolphin's Barn, Dublin 8,* ☎ *453 4153, daily. 19, 19A, 22, 22A buses from city centre to Dolphin's Barn.*
Silver Skate Ice Rink, *North Circular Rd, Dublin 7,* ☎ *830 1263, daily. 19, 34, 38 buses from city centre to Phibsboro'.*

RIDING SCHOOLS AND STABLES
Ashtown Equestrian Centre, *Castleknock, Dublin 15,* ☎ *838 3807.*
Brennanstown Riding School, *Kilmacanogue, Co Wicklow,* ☎ *286 3778.*
Brittas Lodge Riding Stables, *Brittas, Co Wicklow,* ☎ *458 2726.*
Callaighstown Riding Centre, *Rathcoole, Co Dublin* ☎ *458 9236.*

Castleknock Equestrian Centre, *Dublin 15,* ☎ *820 1104.*
Donacomper Riding School, *Celbridge, Co Kildare,* ☎ *628 8221.*
Gormanstown Equestrian Centre, *Balbriggan, Co Dublin,* ☎ *841 2508*
Malahide Riding School, *Ivy Grange, Bloomfield, Dublin 5,* ☎ *846 3622.*

RUGBY
Irish Rugby Football Union (details of matches), *62 Lansdowne Rd, Dublin 4,* ☎ *668 4601.*

SWIMMING POOLS
Ballyfermot, *Le Fanu Park, Dublin 10,* ☎ *626 6504.*
Ballymun, *Ballymun Shopping Centre, Dublin 11,* ☎ *842 1363.*
Bray, *Presentation College, Putland Rd,* ☎ *286 7517/286 2189.*
Clontarf, Open-air sea water pool. *June – Sept.*
Coolock, *Coolock Shopping Centre, Dublin 5,* ☎ *847 7743.*
Crumlin, *Windmill Rd, Dublin 12,* ☎ *455 5792.*
Dun Laoghaire, Open-air sea water pool. *June – Sept.*
Finglas, *Mellowes Rd, Dublin 11,* ☎ *834 8005.*
Loughlinstown, *Leisure Centre, Loughlinstown Drive, Co Dublin,* ☎ *282 3344.*
Monkstown, *Co Dublin,* ☎ *280 7100.*
Rathmines, *Williams Park, Dublin 6,* ☎ *496 1275.*
Sean McDermott St, *Dublin 1,* ☎ *872 0752.*
Townsend St, *Dublin 2,* ☎ *677 0503.*

Except for the open-air pool at Clontarf, all other pools are open on a daily basis. Daily swimming is also available at the Forty Foot (sea bathing), *Sandycove, Co Dublin.*

SOCCER
Football League of Ireland (match details), *80 Merrion Sq, Dublin 2,* ☎ *676 5120.*

SQUASH
Squash Ireland, *Church Rd, Dalkey, Co Dublin,* ☎ *280 8426.*

TENNIS
Tennis Courts (private)
Blackrock Bowling & Tennis Club, *Green Rd, Blackrock,* ☎ *288 1933.*
Castleknock, *Navan Rd, Dublin 15,* ☎ *821 0423.*
Charleville, *Whitworth Rd, Dublin 9,* ☎ *830 4149.*
Donnybrook, *Brookvale Rd, Dublin 4,* ☎ *269 2838.*
Fitzwilliam, *Appian Way, Dublin 6,* ☎ *660 3988.*
Sandycove, *Elton Park, Sandycove, Co Dublin,* ☎ *280 8769.*
Templeogue, *Templeogue Rd, Dublin 6,* ☎ *490 2760.*

Tennis Courts (public)
Belcamp Park, *Darndale, Dublin 5,* ☎ *848 3739.*
Bushy Park, *Terenure, Dublin 6,* ☎ *490 0320.*
Clarinda Park, *Dun Laoghaire,* ☎ *280 9976.*
Eamonn Ceannt Park, *Sundrive Rd, Dublin 12,* ☎ *475 0799.*
Ellenfield Park, *Whitehall, Dublin 9,* ☎ *842 1182.*
Herbert Park, *Ballsbridge, Dublin 4,* ☎ *668 4364.*
Johnstown Park, *Finglas, Dublin 11,* ☎ *834 3656.*
Le Fanu Park, *Ballyfermot, Dublin 10,* ☎ *626 5064.*
Marley Park, *Rathfarnham, Dublin 16,* ☎ *493 4059.*
Mellowes Road Park, *Finglas, Dublin 11,* ☎ *834 6973.*
Poppintree Park, *Ballymun, Dublin 11,* ☎ *842 8833.*
St Anne's Park, *Dollymount, Dublin 3,* ☎ *833 8898.*
Walkinstown Ave, *Walkinstown, Dublin 12,* ☎ *450 3423.*

TEMPLE BAR

The Temple Bar district, which extends from Westmoreland St to Parliament St, and from Dame St to the quays, is a historic part of Dublin city centre that is being transformed through tax incentives into Dublin's cultural quarter. The many new craft and design centres which have set up in the area have earned the district a reputation as Dublin's Left Bank. The area is further enhanced by over 30 restaurants and more than 20 pubs. Further details from the **Temple Bar Information Centre,** *18 Eustace St, Dublin 2,* ☎ *671 5717.*

DESIGNyard, *12 East Essex St, Dublin 2,* ☎ *677 8467.* Applied arts, also jewellery gallery.

Bad Bob's Backstage Bar, *34 East Essex St, Dublin 2* ☎ *679 2992.* Irish, country and Cajun music.

Gallery of Photography, *33-34 East Essex St, Dublin 2* ☎ *671 4654.*

Graphic Studio Gallery, *8A Cope St, Dublin 2* ☎ *679 8021.* Contemporary art.

Green Building, *3-4 Crow St/23-24 Temple Lane, Dublin 2.* The "greenest" place in Ireland, using green technology to its utmost for heating and lighting.

Original Print Gallery, *4 Temple Bar,* ☎ *677 3657.* Contemporary art.

Peter Hogan Gallery, *57 Dame St, Dublin 2,* ☎ *677 0363.* Contemporary art.

Irish Film Centre, *6 Eustace St, Dublin 2,* ☎ *679 3477.* Two cinemas, film archives, bookshop, bar, restaurant.

Poddle Bridge. New curved bridge is planned, to connect the district with the North quays on opposite side of the river, complementing the Ha'penny Bridge, a long-established Dublin landmark.

Project Arts Centre, *39 East Essex St, Dublin 2* ☎ *671 2321.* Contemporary theatre, exhibitions.

Thomas Read & Co, *4 Parliament St, Dublin 2* ☎ *677 1487.* This cutlery shop is Dublin's oldest retailer, founded 1670.

The Kitchen Nightclub, *Clarence Hotel, Wellington Quay, Dublin 2,* ☎ *677 6178.*

Wyvern Gallery, *2 Temple Lane, Dublin 2,* ☎ *679 9589.* Contemporary art.

Viking Museum (planned). Due to open in former St Michael & St John's church, facing the river.

RESTAURANTS

The Alamo, *19 Temple Bar.* Mexican restaurant with tacos, burritos and Chimi-Changas; all very mouth- and eye-watering stuff.

Big Fish, *corner Wellington Quay and Eustace Street.* Intriguing menu mix includes buffalo wings, crab sandwiches, seafood pasta and veal rissole.

Café Gertrude, *Bedford Row, off Temple Bar.* Light and airy café serving snacks and salads.

Elephant and Castle, *18 Temple Bar,* ☎ *679 3121.* Black and white façade, wooden chairs and tables inside, wide-ranging menu includes New York jumbo sandwiches and omelettes.

Little Lisbon, *2 Fownes Street, Dublin 2* ☎ *671 1274.* Claimed to be Ireland's first authentic, traditional Portuguese restaurant, with plenty of fish on the menu. Also Brazilian style cooking. Brightly decorated tablecloths complement the fishing nets that hang from the ceiling.

La Paloma, *Asdill's Row, off Temple Bar,* ☎ *677 7392.* Authentic Spanish cuisine. Daytime menu includes tapas, while main dishes include tortilla española.

La Pigalle, *14 Temple Bar,* ☎ *671 9262.* French-style cuisine and ambiance for lunch and dinner.

TRANSPORT

BICYCLE HIRE

The following is a list of bicycle hire companies. The weekly rate is around £25; a deposit of about £35 is normally required.

The Cycle Centre, *Unit 7, Old Bawn Shopping Centre, Tallaght,* ☎ *451 8771.*

Joe Daly, *Rosemount, Dundrum, Dublin 14,* ☎ *298 1485.*

Hardings, *30 Bachelor's Walk, Dublin 1,* ☎ *873 2455.*

E. R. Harris & Son, *87C Greenpark Rd, also 78 Main St, Bray, Co Wicklow,* ☎ *286 3357/286 7995.*

Hollingsworth, *56 Templeogue Village, Dublin 6W,* ☎ *490 5094, 1 Drummartin Rd, Lower Kilmacud Rd, Co Dublin,* ☎ *296 0255.*

Little Sport, *3 Merville Ave, Fairview, Dublin 3,* ☎ *833 2405.*

McDonald's Cycles, *38 Wexford St, Dublin 2,* ☎ *475 2586.*
Mikes Bikes, *Unit 6, St George's Mall, Dun Laoghaire Shopping Centre,* ☎ *280 0417.*
Ray's Bike Shop, *2 Milltown Centre, Milltown, Dublin 6,* ☎ *283 0355.*
Rent a Bike, *58 Lower Gardiner St, Dublin 1,* ☎ *872 5399.*

BUSES
City-centre departure points:
Aston Quay, *50, 56A, 77B, 78A.*
Beresford Place, *27B, 42, 53.*
Burgh Quay, *14, 14A, 79.*
College St, *15A, 15B, 55.*
Crampton Quay, *49, 49A, 65, 65A, 65B.*
Eden Quay, *5, 7, 8, 20A, 20B, 33, 41, 41A, 41C, 45, 54A, 60, 63, 84.*
Fleet St (both parts), *21A, 46A, 51, 51B, 51C, 86.*
Hawkins St, *44, 47, 47A, 48A, 62.*
Lower Abbey St, *28, 29A, 30, 31, 31B, 32, 32A, 32B, 37, 38, 44A, 44B, 70.*
Lower Gardiner St, *27, 27A.*
Middle Abbey St, *25, 25A, 26, 34, 39, 66, 66A, 67, 67A.*
Parnell Sq, *36, 36A.*
Parnell St, *40, 40A, 40B, 40C.*
Talbot St, *42B.*
Wellington Quay, *49A, 65, 65A, 65B.*

In addition, the following cross-city buses go via O'Connell St, *3, 10, 11, 11A, 11B, 13, 16, 16A, 19, 19A, 22, 22A, 90.* All provincial buses depart from Busarus, Store St, Dublin 1. Airport buses depart from Heuston mainline rail station and Busarus.

BUS AND COACH TOURS
Dublin City
Bus Átha Cliath (Dublin Bus), *59 Upper O'Connell St, Dublin 1,* ☎ *873 4222.*

Bus Éireann, ☎ *836 6111.*
Gogan Travel, *7 South Great George's St, Dublin 2,* ☎ *679 6444.*
Gray Line Dublin City Tours, *3 Clanwilliam Terrace, Grand Canal Quay, Dublin 2,* ☎ *661 9666.*
Bus Éireann operates city-bus tours departing from Upper O'Connell St and Busarus daily in summer, three times a week in winter. Dublin Bus operates an open-topped bus on tours of the city daily, all year, except for Sundays in winter. Frequency varies with demand. Gogan Travel runs conducted coach tours of Dublin city, with Eamonn MacThomais as narrator, on Sundays all year and several times a week in summer.

Outside Dublin
Bus Éireann, *59 Upper O'Connell St, Dublin 1,* ☎ *836 6111.*
Furlong Tours, *Sandyford Rd, Dublin 14,* ☎ *295 6254.*
Gray Line Tours, *see above.*
Bus Éireann tours include the following destinations, from Easter–September: New Ross, Doonaree Forest Park, Co Cavan, the Boyne Valley and Newgrange, Vale of Avoca and Glendalough. Gray Line Tours runs tours to Malahide Castle, Glendalough, Co Wicklow, the Hill of Tara and the Boyne Valley, including Newgrange, and river cruises on the River Shannon. Furlong Tours runs tours to Newgrange and other country tourist destinations.

CAR HIRE
The cheapest weekly rate for car hire, with unlimited mileage and including comprehensive insurance, is about £100/£200. For advice on car hire contact Car Rental Council, *5 Upper Pembroke St, Dublin 2,* ☎ *676 1690/676 6332. The following is a list of car hire companies.*
Argus, *19 Terenure Park, Dublin 6,* ☎ *490 4444.*
Avis/Johnson & Perrott, *1 Hanover St East, Dublin 2,* ☎ *677 4010.*
Cahill Motors, *Dublin 5,* ☎ *831 4066.*

Flynn Bros Budget Rent-a-Car, *Dublin airport,* ☎ *842 0793.*
Hertz Rent-a-Car, *Hertz House, Leeson St Bridge, Dublin 4,* ☎ *660 2255. Dublin airport,* ☎ *842 9333. Dun Laoghaire ferryport,* ☎ *280 1518.*
Irish Car Rentals, *Dublin airport,* ☎ *844 4900, Duke St, Dublin 2,* ☎ *679 9420.*
Murray's, *Baggot St Bridge, Dublin 4,* ☎ *668 1777, Dublin airport,* ☎ *844 4179, 12 Upper O'Connell St,* ☎ *874 5844.*
O'Mara's Rent-a-Car, *Dublin airport,* ☎ *842 9313.*
South County Self-Drive, *Rochestown Ave, Dun Laoghaire, Co Dublin,* ☎ *280 6005.*
Windsor Rent-a-Car, *South Circular Rd, Dublin 8,* ☎ *454 0800.*

Useful Addresses
Automobile Association, *23 Rock Hill, Blackrock,* ☎ *283 3555.* Reciprocal insurance arrangements in case of emergency for members of foreign touring/motoring clubs.
Emergency Car Breakdown Service, Automobile Association, *23 Suffolk St, Dublin 2,* ☎ *677 9481.*
Irish Visiting Motorists' Bureau, *5 South Frederick St, Dublin 2,* ☎ *679 7233.* Insurance help for motorists from outside Ireland in case of accident or insurance.
Royal Irish Automobile Club, *34 Dawson St, Dublin 2,* ☎ *677 5141.*

TAXI
Dublin has nearly 100 private taxi operators (individuals and firms). Main operators include Blue Cabs, ☎ *676 1111, Devlin Metro Cabs,* ☎ *668 3333, National Radio Cabs,* ☎ *677 2222, VIP,* ☎ *678 3333. Taxi fares range from £2.00 to £10.00, depending on length of journey. Asterisks at the end of entries denote a 24-hr service.*

Taxi Ranks
Amiens St, *Dublin 1,* ☎ *874 3288.*
Angle, *Ranelagh, Dublin 6,* ☎ *497 2735.* *

Burlington Hotel, *Dublin 4,* ☎ *676 4107.* *
College Green, *Dublin 2,* ☎ *677 7440.* *
Crescent, *Malahide Rd, Dublin 3,* ☎ *833 6507.* *
Dun Laoghaire, *Co Dublin,* ☎ *280 5263.* *
Lansdowne Rd, *Dublin 4,* ☎ *661 7222.* *
O'Connell St (opp. Easons), *Dublin 1,* ☎ *878 6150.* *
Raheny Village, *Dublin 5,* ☎ *831 6699.*
Rathmines Rd Upper, *Dublin 6,* ☎ *497 3276.* *
St Stephen's Green (2 ranks), *Dublin 2,* ☎ *676 2847/676 7381.* *
Terenure Rd North, *Dublin 6,* ☎ *490 1860.* *

TRAINS

In the greater Dublin area, the fast and frequent DART electric service links Bray with Howth, via Pearse, Tara Street and Connolly stations. The journey time for the entire line is about one hour. In addition to the DART service, a fast, frequent service connects all stations between Dundalk and Arklow. New commuter services are running on two lines. From Connolly station, Dublin, a service runs to Broombridge, Ashtown, Blanchardstown/Castleknock, Coolmine, Clonsilla, Leixlip and Maynooth. A second fast new commuter service runs from Heuston station to Cherry Orchard, Clondalkin, Hazelhatch/Celbridge, Sallins and Naas, Newbridge and Kildare. There is also a connecting train service between the DART terminus at Bray and Greystones. Dublin is also the starting point for all mainline railway services, which operate out of two principal stations: Connolly, for the north, north-west and east, and Heuston for the west, south, south-west and south-east. Telephone enquiries for all rail services, including DART, ☎ *836 6222.*
Connolly Station, *Amiens St, Dublin 1,* ☎ *836 3333.*
Heuston Station, *Kingsbridge, Dublin 8,* ☎ *836 3333.*
DART trains run from approximately 7 a.m. until 11.30 p.m., Monday to Sunday. At peak rush-hour periods, Monday to Friday, trains run every 5–10 minutes in each direction. At other times, the interval between trains is up to 20 minutes.

From Connolly and Pearse stations, Westland Row, there are

mainline trains, about four a day in each direction, to Dun Laoghaire, Bray, Wicklow, Arklow, Wexford and Rosslare. Also from Connolly station there are departures to Mullingar and Sligo, and to Dundalk, Newry, Lurgan, Portadown and Belfast Central. There are about six departures a day in each direction.

From Heuston station, there are departures to Athy, Ballina, Carlow, Charleville, Cork, Galway, Kildare, Kilkenny, Killarney, Limerick, Mallow, Nenagh, Newbridge, Portarlington, Portlaoise, Roscrea, Thurles, Tralee, Waterford and Westport. On all mainline services, there are at least three trains a day in each direction.

UNUSUAL EXCURSIONS

Unusual excursions in the Dublin area are centred on the use of public transport, both bus and DART.

Blessington, *Co Wicklow.* takes about 1½ hrs to traverse delightful Wicklow countryside to this village with French-style main street. *65 bus from Crampton Quay, city centre.*

Bohernabreena. A wonderful bus excursion, especially in early summer. Located in foothills of the Dublin Mountains, near a major reservoir. Journey there will show much of S Dublin suburbs. *49A bus from Aston Quay, city centre. Journey time: about 1 hr.*

Chapelizod to Lucan. Follow the minor road that hugs the N bank of the River Liffey for *5 km (3 miles)* between the the two villages. Your meander will start by the Strawberry Beds, a popular holiday place for Dubliners in years gone by. *25, 26, 66, 66A, 67, 67A buses from city centre to Chapelizod.*

Coliemore Harbour, Dalkey to Dalkey Island. Frequent boat trips in summer, no advance booking. Island has ruins of old church, military barracks, Martello tower. Also goat herd. *8 bus to Dalkey village, then 10 mins walk to harbour.* DART *to Dalkey stations then 10 mins walk.*

Delgany. 84 bus from city centre through Bray and Greystones to Delgany, an unspoiled village with three hostelries and excellent surrounding walks. *Journey time: 1½ hrs.*

Dockland. Tour of Custom House quay, North Wall and other parts of Dublin's dockland. *53A bus from Beresford Place (beside Liberty Hall). Allow 1½ hrs for round trip.*

Dublin Airport. A hive of activity day and night. Viewing terraces to see planes landing and taking off, bars, restaurants, craft and gift shops. *Airport bus from main railway stations and Busarus, also 41A, 230 buses from city centre.*

Dublin South. 17 bus from Blackrock to Rialto gives fascinating glimpses of much of S and SW Dublin in all its varying patterns and landscapes. *One way journey time: 1½ hrs.*

Glencullen. A small, delightful village at an elevated location in the Dublin Mountains. Little to do, but excellent views. *44B bus from city centre. Infrequent service (seven on weekdays, six on Saturdays, none on Sundays). Journey time: 1¼ hrs.*

Ireland's Eye. Summer boat excursions from Howth Harbour, *0.8 km (0.5 mile). Daily, by arr,* ☎ *831 4200.* DART *to Howth Village. Journey time: 20 mins.*

Killiney Village. Superb views down to Bray and Bray Head from small, hilltop village with interesting pubs and restaurants. DART *to Dun Laoghaire station, then 59 bus.*

Lighthouse. Number 3 bus from city centre to Ringsend and new electricity generating station. Walk from Poolbeg extension terminus to lighthouse. *Allow 3 hrs for round trip.*

Mountains. 47 bus from city centre ambles through S Dublin suburbs, then climbs into foothills of Dublin Mountains, culminating at Tibradden and Rockbrook. *Allow 3 hrs for round trip.*

North Dublin/Meath. 70 bus from Middle Abbey St, city centre, crosses interesting part of NW Dublin, Ashtown and Castleknock before heading out into Mulhuddart and Dunboyne, an attractive rural part of S Co Meath.

North Co Dublin. 33 bus from Eden Quay, city centre, takes in major centres in N county: Swords, Lusk, Rush, Skerries, Balbriggan. Return from Balbriggan by train. *Journey time: about 1½ hrs.*

Sutton to Howth. By means of the 31B bus from Sutton railway station. The journey used to be done by Ireland's last surviving tram service; one of those trams is in Howth transport museum. *Journey time: 30 mins.*

Sutton to Malahide. Coastal meander through Baldoyle and Portmarnock by DART feeder bus No. 102 from Sutton station and vice versa.

Wicklow Town. Attractive walks in harbour area. *Bus from Busarus or train from Connolly/Pearse station. Journey time: 1 hr.*

WALKS

Walking (or cycling) is the best means of seeing the innumerable attractions of Dublin and its surrounding region. Where applicable, details are given of public transport to the starting point of these walks. Approximate times and distances are given for the walks.

Baldoyle to Portmarnock. Bracing coastal road walk, with good views of Ireland's Eye, culminating in Portmarnock's fine strand, one of the Dublin area's best beaches. DART *to Baldoyle, return by 32, 32A buses from Portmarnock. About 5 km (3 miles).*

Ballycorus. Mountain area walks W of Kilternan on Dublin-Enniskerry road, R117. See also ruins of ancient lead mine. *2 hrs.*

Barnaslingan. *10 km (6 miles) S of Dundrum on R117 road to Enniskerry.* Forest walks adjacent to the Scalp Mountain; scenic views. *44 bus from city centre. Journey time: 1 hr.*

Booterstown Ave/Mount Merrion Ave. This part of S Co Dublin provides safe, secluded walking territory in one of Dun Laoghaire borough's most fashionable residential districts. *5, 7, 8, 45 buses from city centre to Booterstown.* DART *to Booterstown, 300 metres to Booterstown Ave. 1 hr.*

Bull Wall. Walk along embankment that stretches into Dublin Bay, giving one of the city's most bracing walks. *30 bus from city centre to Clontarf Rd. 3 km (2 miles). 1½ hrs.*

Chapelizod. From the village, there's a steep climb up Knockmaroon Hill into the Phoenix Park, giving good views of the Liffey Valley. The walk can be continued through to Castleknock village. *25, 26, 66, 66A, 67, 67A buses from city centre to Chapelizod. About 2.5 km (1.5 miles). 1½ hrs.*

Clanbrassil St. Atmospheric and interesting, despite its dereliction. To immediate W is a district called the Tenters, because Huguenot settlers wove linen here and hung it to dry. *49, 49A, 54, 54A buses from city centre to top of Clanbrassil St. 1½ hrs.*

Cruagh Wood, *8 km (5 miles) S of Rathfarnham on R115 road.* Forest walks, nature trail, wilderness trek. *3 hrs.*

Custom House Quay to North Wall Quay. N side of River Liffey is main docks area. The Custom House quay area is being developed as a financial services area, with many ancillary facilities, such as cinemas, museums, restaurants. *3 km (2 miles). 1 hr.*

Dalkey. One of the best walks in Dublin area, from Bulloch Harbour, through centre of village, up Coliemore Rd (hotel ideal for refreshment break), past Coliemore Harbour, into small seaside park, up to Vico Rd with excellent views over Killiney Bay and Bray Head. *8 bus from Dublin to Bulloch Harbour. About 3 km (2 miles). 1½ hrs. Also DART to Dalkey station.*

Dublin Castle to Kevin Street. S of the castle, there's a whole warren of run-down streets, some of Dublin's oldest. From Ship St, through Golden Lane to Bride St and Kevin St, the district is quite captivating. *1 hr.*

Dublin's Georgian Area. Interesting walk, starting in Merrion Sq, going up Lower Fitzwilliam St (ignoring ESB head office monstrosity that replaced fine Georgian terrace), into Upper Fitzwilliam St and Fitzwilliam Sq. Happily, it is now much more fashionable to preserve rather than destroy Georgian buildings, so the area remains in good order. *1 hr.*

Dublin Markets. From Capel St, go along Mary St Little or Mary's Abbey to the markets area. Old area of Dublin has great character, while the markets themselves are peopled with characters. *1 hr.*

Dublin's Liberties. Starting at Christchurch Cathedral and walking along Thomas St into James's St gives a lively insight into one of the city's oldest and most individualistic areas. Many side streets off the main thoroughfare are equally interesting. Continue past Guinness brewery into Basin St: the brewery's Grand Canal terminus is filled in, but some of the area's atmosphere remains. *About 3 km (2 miles). 1½ hrs.*

Five Lamps, *Dublin 1.* Interesting walks in this rather derelict, but historically interesting, part of Dublin's northside, taking in North Strand, up to Summerhill and Ballybough Rd. *20A, 20B, 30, 44A buses from city centre to North Strand. 1 hr.*

Grand Canal. Charming walk along the banks of the Grand Canal, starting at Baggot St bridge, passing the seat dedicated to Patrick Kavanagh the poet. Continue across Leeson St bridge as far as Charlemont St bridge. Particularly striking walk in autumn. *30 mins.*

Hell Fire Club. On Dublin Mountains, *6 km (4 miles),* S of Rathfarnham on R116 road. Ruins of club, noted for 18th c sorcery. Excellent mountainside walks and views over Dublin. *2 hrs.*

Manor St. This area of NW Dublin has changed little in the last 80 years. Walk through district gives excellent impression of Joycean Dublin, yet it's one of the least heralded districts of the city. *37, 39, 70 buses from city centre. 1 hr.*

Massey's Wood, *6 km (4 miles) S of Rathfarnham on R115 road to Glencree.* Forest Walks. *1 hr.*

Pearse St to Ringsend. Starting at the Waterways Visitor Centre in Grand Canal basin, it takes in industrial buildings, such as Boland's Mills (a 1916 stronghold) and the 1930s Art Deco Bovril factory through to the grimy but interesting Ringsend district. Continue through Irishtown to Sandymount Strand. *About 5 km (3 miles). 1½ hrs.*

Poolbeg Lighthouse. Bracing walk from ESB electricity generating station at Ringsend along wall to Poolbeg lighthouse. Plenty of fresh air, good views of Dublin Bay. *3 bus to Ringsend. 2.5 km (1.5 miles). 1½ hrs.*

Ranelagh. Two of Dublin's lesser-known squares, Dartmouth and Mountpleasant, just S of Grand Canal, provide excellent walks in quiet residential area. *44, 48A, 62, 86 buses from city centre to Ranelagh Rd. 1 hr.*

River Dodder. From the bridge at Ballsbridge, you can follow the riverside path almost to the sea. Quiet, undemanding walk. *5, 7, 8, 45 buses to Ballsbridge,* DART *to Lansdowne Rd station. 2.5 km (1.5 miles). 1½ hrs.*

River Dodder Linear Park. Excellent riverside walks. From Clonskeagh Rd to Dartry, *1.5 km (1 mile).* Then from Dartry Rd to Bushy Park, *2.5 km (1.5 miles),* the walk is even more rewarding. *11, 62 buses from city centre to Clonskeagh Rd (O'Shea's pub). 2 hrs.*

River Liffey Quays. Starting at George's Quay, by Butt bridge, there is a fascinating walk down along the quays, as far as Britain Quay. *About 2.5 km (2 miles). 1 hr.* Sadly, the passenger ferry no longer plies across the Liffey from Ringsend.

Going upstream, if you start at Aston Quay (O'Connell bridge) and go W your journey is dotted with many interesting craft and other shops. Between Christchurch Cathedral and the river, the Wood Quay site has been filled in by the vast Dublin Corporation buildings, recently and dramatically extended. The quay walk can be continued as far as Heuston station. The nearby Ryan's pub, splendid in its untouched Victoriana, is a fitting journey's end. *3 km (2 miles). 1½ hrs.*

Sandymount Green. Pleasant green space lined by interesting food, antique and other shops. Short walk to Sandymount strand. *3, 18 buses to Sandymount Green.* DART *to Sandymount, 500 metres. ½ hr.*

Sutton Cross to Howth via Howth Summit. One of the most testing walks in the Dublin area; steep climb from Sutton village to summit. Alternative route from Howth summit to Howth village by cliff walk; more dangerous, but more exciting. *31 bus from city centre to Sutton & Howth.* DART *to Sutton & Howth. 31B bus from city centre to summit. About 9 km (6 miles).*

Temple Bar Area of Central Dublin. Between Dame St and River Liffey, this historic area, full of narrow streets, unusual shops and some interesting restaurants, is being regenerated into Dublin's own Left Bank. *1 hr.*

Tibradden, *about 8 km (5 miles) S of Rathfarnham on R116 road* to Glencullen. Attractive forest walks with climb to mountain summit. *47 bus from city centre to Tibradden. 3 hrs.*

Trinity College. Walk through the college grounds, from the front gate, through the sports grounds, to Lincoln Place. An oasis of calm in the city centre. ½ hr.

University College, Dublin. Belfield grounds off Stillorgan Rd provide spacious walking areas. However, caution advised at night. *10 bus from city centre to* UCD *terminus. 1hr.*

Wellington Rd, *Ballsbridge.* One of Dublin's widest and most elegant roads, together with neighbouring Clyde Rd, Raglan Rd and a host of lanes, provides an unusual suburban walk. *10, 46A buses to Wellington Rd. About 3 km (2 miles). 1 hr.*

306